Rise Above

Transforming Work Stress into Success

By
Leah DeMarest

Copyright 2024 Leah DeMarest. All rights reserved. ISBN: 9798218530464

No part of this book may be reproduced in any form or by any electronic or mechanical means including information storage and retrieval systems, without permission in writing from the author. The only exception is by a reviewer, who may quote short excerpts in a review.

Although the author and publisher have made every effort to ensure that the information in this book was correct at press time, the author and publisher do not assume and hereby disclaim any liability to any party for any loss, damage, or disruption caused by errors or omissions, whether such errors or omissions result from negligence, accident, or any other cause.

This publication is designed to provide accurate and authoritative information with regard to the subject matter covered. It is sold with the understanding that the publisher is not engaged in rendering professional services. If legal advice or other expert assistance is required, the services of a competent professional should be sought.

The fact that an organization or website is referred to in this work as a citation and/or a potential source of further information does not mean that the author or the publisher endorses the information the organization or website may provide or recommendations it may make.

Please remember that Internet websites listed in this work may have changed or disappeared between when this work was written and when it is read.

Rise Above

Transforming Work Stress into Success

Table of Contents

Introduction 1

Chapter 1: Understanding Work Stress 5

Chapter 2: Strategies to Cope with
Overwhelming Feelings 20

Chapter 3: Achieving Focus Amidst Distractions 36

Chapter 4: Mastering Your To-Do List 52

Chapter 5: Motivation Maintenance 67

Chapter 6: Stress Reduction Techniques 85

Chapter 7: Navigating Interpersonal
Challenges at Work 102

Chapter 8: Securing Your Worth:
Asking for a Raise 118

Chapter 9: Advocating for Workplace
Accommodations 132

Chapter 10: Bringing Ideas to the Forefront 146

Chapter 11: Influencing Workplace
Policies and Procedures 161

Chapter 12: Balancing the Scales:
Work-Life Integration 177

Chapter 13: Putting It All Together:
A Roadmap to Well-Being 194

Chapter 14: Staying Agile: Adapting to
Changing Work Environments 211

Chapter 15: Cultivating a Positive
Workplace Culture 226

Conclusion 242

Appendix A: Additional Resources
for Managing Work Stress 246
   A.1: Recommended Reading 246
   A.2: Stress-Management Apps and Tools 251
   A.3: Professional Organizations
   for Stress and Well-Being 257

Introduction

Welcome to a journey that traverses the often challenging landscape of the modern workplace. Within these pages lies a roadmap to uncovering the joy of our labor, ensuring fruitful productivity, and navigating the intricate balance between professional demands and personal fulfillment. This expedition is not about altering the essence of who we are, but rather about embracing and harnessing our unique traits and experiences to find satisfaction in our work.

You'll find that this book isn't just about coping with stress; it's a deep-dive exploration into the personal and professional strategies that foster well-being and happiness. We delve into the principles of managing the inevitable pressure and demands that accompany our careers, and how to emerge not just unscathed, but thriving.

We begin by grounding ourselves in an understanding of work stress. It's a complex beast that often lurks in the shadows of our professional lives. Rather than shy away, we'll confront it head-on, dissecting its anatomy and recognizing the triggers that set our nerves on edge. By comprehending the root of our stress, we empower ourselves to address it with intelligence and grace.

Armed with the knowledge of what rattles us, we then pivot to the arsenal of strategies available to compose ourselves when overwhelmed. Here, we learn the subtle art of breathing life into tranquility through mindfulness and positive self-affirmation, setting boundaries to protect our energy and spirit like cherished artifacts in a museum.

As we progress further, focus becomes our watchword. The dust storms of distraction have no claim over us as we determine what deserves our attention the most, wielding the magic of single-minded determination to accomplish tasks with a surgeon's precision.

Yet, what of the mountainous to-do lists that seem to grow like mythical hydras? We tackle this beast not with mythical swords but with the pragmatic tools of breaking down gargantuan tasks, technology's assistance, and the judicious deployment of delegation – an art unto itself.

Motivation can be as elusive as a mirage, but it need not be. By setting milestones and drawing from the well of personal goals, we find the sustenance to keep climbing, step by incremental step, towards our aspirations.

When the weight of stress attempts to pull us down, we have techniques at our beck and call to lift the burdens. From the cathartic release offered by physical exercise to the wisdom of taking pauses that punctuate our daily grind, we keep our mental engines running smooth and steady.

But what of the unpredictable ecosystem of office relationships? Even amidst thorny coworkers and challenging superiors, we can navigate with diplomatic finesse and conflict resolution skills that preserve our integrity and serenity.

Recognizing our worth extends beyond mere self-assurance—it's about ensuring that others see our value too. Thus, when we speak of securing raises or workplace accommodations, it's with the understanding that such quests are done with preparedness, timing, and an unwavering belief in our own merit.

We are not idle players in the grand stage of our workplaces. We have voices that should echo in the halls, presenting ideas with persuasive vigor and championing changes that align with our vision of an ideal professional environment.

This book isn't just a guide; it's a reflection of our collective experiences, reminding us that work and life are not antagonistic forces but partners in a dance. It's in the elegant waltz between the two that we find true harmony, leveraging strategies to manage time and cultivate passions that enrich us beyond the office walls.

Ultimately, we'll synthesize these countless threads into a coherent tapestry—a personal plan for stress management that invites routine but is pliable enough to accommodate the inevitable shifts of life and career.

Because the world of work is ever-evolving, agility is not just an asset—it's a necessity. By fostering an attitude that embraces change, learns continually, and eyes the future with a bright spark of optimism, we become not just survivors of this corporate ecosystem, but its pioneers.

Last, we cannot ignore the fertile soil from which a healthy workplace culture sprouts. It's here that we have the opportunity to sow the seeds of communal wellness and support, nurturing a garden where everyone can flourish. Through leadership, encouragement, and the establishment of a sustaining network, we contribute to a legacy that goes beyond mere job titles and paychecks—it's about creating an enduring, positive impact.

And so, with each page turned, we invite you to dive with us into these vibrant waters, explore the depths of your professional potential, and emerge with newfound clarity and purpose. For in the journey to happiness at work, the true destination is ourselves.

Chapter 1:
Understanding Work Stress

As we delve into the complexities of work stress, it's essential to begin with a foundational understanding of its makeup. Within the whirlwind of deadlines, team dynamics, and ever-growing to-do lists, stress can arise from multiple facets of our professional lives. This stress, while commonplace, mustn't be dismissed as the necessary price of success. Instead, we should scrutinize its anatomy—examining how the pressures of productivity, the weight of expectations, and the fast pace of the modern work environment converge to challenge our mental and emotional equilibrium.

The first step to mastering work stress lies in recognizing your personal stress triggers. Identifying these triggers requires a thoughtful and honest assessment of your workday. Which tasks consistently generate anxiety? What interactions leave you feeling drained? And, most importantly, how do your own thoughts and perceptions about work contribute to these feelings of stress? It's through this understanding that we begin to chart a course towards healthier work experiences. By pinpointing these triggers, we position ourselves to respond rather than react—a subtle but transformative shift in managing workplace challenges.

The role of perception in work stress cannot be understated. Our interpretation of events shapes our emotional and physiological responses. When faced with a tight deadline, one might see an insurmountable obstacle, while another perceives an opportunity to excel. It's this lens through which we view our professional lives that often dictates the level of stress we experience. Nurturing a mindset that seeks constructive outcomes and learns from setbacks is crucial in reframing the challenges that work presents and mitigating the feelings of being overwhelmed.

While subsequent chapters of this book will offer strategies to cope with stress and promote balance, this initial chapter establishes the ground on which these techniques will build. By understanding the breadth and depth of work stress, we are better prepared to implement the practical advice that follows. It's not merely about surviving the workday but transforming our relationship with work so that it becomes a source of satisfaction and fulfillment, not unceasing stress.

In essence, grasping the subtle contours of work stress is akin to mapping an uncharted territory. The terrain might be tough, but the journey is rewarding. As you continue through this book, keep in mind that understanding is the precursor to change, and an in-depth exploration of work stress is the first solid step towards a happier and more balanced professional life.

The Anatomy of Work Stress is a concept that can be elusive yet omnipresent, a paradox that many of us grapple with daily. It is a fabric woven from numerous threads: expectations, demands, and personal perceptions of our workplace. When these threads bind together without relief, the fabric can suffocate.

It begins, quite often, with a seed; a single, subtle nudge outside one's comfort zone. This might be an upcoming deadline, an overbearing supervisor, or an email brimming with critique. It's the initial heartbeat of discomfort, one that's easily dismissed yet lays the groundwork for a more insidious narrative.

As the seed takes root, it is nourished by repetition. The continuous drip of tight deadlines becomes a storm, the once manageable assignments grow in number and complexity, and suddenly, the balance tips. The body's fight-or-flight response kicks in, but in the modern workspace, neither option is typically constructive. Instead, we're left oscillating between them, trapped in a cycle of heightened anxiety and stress.

Understand that stress has different faces, presenting as psychological pressure, physical fatigue or as a disquiet that disrupts our emotional equilibrium. Each of these experiences has its own biological and psychological impacts that can mar the mind's clarity and the body's vitality, often manifesting in a myriad of symptoms, from headaches to irritability, to a decrease in productivity.

Interpersonal relationships at work can further complicate the anatomy of work stress. Colleagues with competing interests, communication breakdowns, and challenging dynamics can turn collaborative projects into battlegrounds. In such arenas, our desire for belonging clashes with the need for self-preservation, leading to an emotional tug-of-war that can leave us feeling drained and conflicted.

Resource limitations pose another layer of complexity. Scarcity, whether in terms of time, help, or material support, often means heavier workloads fall on fewer shoulders. It's a suffocating circumstance when one feels buried beneath the weight of expectations with no relief in sight.

Technology, with all its benefits, brings with it a paradox. Being connected means work can follow us home, blurring lines tightly drawn before. The dings of work emails and messages during family dinners or late at night serve as constant reminders that work is never truly left at the office.

What's nuanced about work stress is its uniquely personal nature. Two individuals can face identical circumstances and experience vastly different levels of stress. This difference is rooted in individual resilience, past experiences, personal life circumstances, as well as one's coping mechanisms and perception of control over their situation.

The stage upon which stress unfolds is also significant. Organizational culture influences how stress is expressed and managed. In cultures where 'busy' is worn as a badge of honor, employees may push themselves beyond healthy limits. In contrast, workplaces that prioritize well-being may mitigate stress through supportive policies and open dialogue.

The cumulative effect of work stress can steal life's flavors. Burnout, a state of emotional, physical, and mental exhaustion, is the cliff one teeters on when chronic stress is left unchecked. It's the body's way of saying, "No more," a state where even the simplest tasks become herculean efforts.

Yet stress is also a messenger, if we listen closely. It tells us when boundaries have been breached, when needs aren't met, and when change is necessary. It calls for reflection, for understanding one's limits and triggers. Through understanding stress, one can begin to navigate through its winding corridors towards well-being.

Physiologically, work stress can activate the sympathetic nervous system, releasing stress hormones like cortisol and adrenaline. Though designed to aid survival, persistent activation of this system wreaks havoc on our health, from weakening our immune system to increasing the risk of chronic diseases.

Cognitively, stress hijacks our mental faculties. Decision-making falters, attention scatters, and creativity withers. It's a state akin to looking through a fogged lens, where clear thoughts and sharp focus become elusive commodities.

Emotionally, the effects of work stress may dip one into a well of blues. Joy can be dimmed by the shadow of anxiety or depression, and even when the office is left behind, the emotional residue can taint life beyond work, affecting relationships and personal contentment.

In deliberating on the anatomy of work stress, one comes to discern that it's not just about workloads and deadlines. It's as though we're juggling, constantly adding more to what we're balancing, all while we're expected to smile and keep pace. Ironically, it's often when one feels they can't afford to stop and assess their stress that they need to do it most critically.

To grasp the full scope of work stress is to map the terrain of our professional lives. We must acknowledge its topography—the peaks of acute stress and the valleys of despondency. Only by understanding can we begin to untangle the threads of stress, to weave a more resilient tapestry for ourselves, to not merely survive the workday but thrive within it.

Recognizing Your Stress Triggers

Embarking on the path toward happiness and serenity at work, understanding what ignites the flames of stress is a critical step. Stress triggers, or stimuli that spark a stress response, differ from individual to individual and might seem as elusive as shadows that move just out of direct view. Recognizing these triggers is an intricate process, requiring us to look inward and acknowledge the external factors that affect our internal balance.

Imagine for a moment the variety of situations that unfold in a workday. An overflowing inbox, a critical email, a looming deadline, or even interpersonal dynamics with colleagues can serve as catalysts for stress. To begin mapping out these triggers, it is valuable to maintain a journal over the course of a week or two. Noting down situations that bring on feelings of stress provides tangible evidence of patterns that you might not be immediately aware of.

It's important to note that stress triggers can be both acute, such as an unexpected confrontation, and chronic, like enduring dissatisfaction with your role. While some triggers are blatant, others are more subtle, perhaps manifested in a slowly building sense of angst as a project progresses. As you reflect on the stressors documented in your journal, you might identify certain trends. Perhaps it's not the volume of work, but rather the nature of tasks or the environment in which they are performed that are the true culprits of your unease.

Another avenue for uncovering stress triggers is through mindfulness. As you tune into your present experience, notice your physical reactions in stressful moments. A tight chest, rapid heartbeat, or quickened breath can serve as bodily cues. Mindfulness helps anchor you in the now and provides clarity, allowing the subtle details of your reactions to come to the forefront.

It is also vital to examine how your perception plays a role—our interpretation of events can either magnify or diminish our stress response. Identifying if you tend to catastrophize or overestimate threats in the workplace can illuminate why seemingly minor events trigger outsized stress reactions. Recognizing that perception is malleable offers a glimpse into how cognitive restructuring could alleviate some of the impacts of these triggers.

Looking past the immediate, consider your foundational beliefs about work. Do you see it as a place where you must perform flawlessly, where failure is not an option? Such rigid thinking can transform even the smallest tasks into stress triggers. Challenging these beliefs and embracing a growth mindset can transform your workplace into a setting for development and learning, instead of a minefield of potential failures.

Commit to having open dialogues about stressors with trusted peers or mentors. Whether it's over a coffee break or a more formal meeting, discussing the situations that trigger stress can help validate your experiences and bring clarity. Others might share their own strategies or even offer insights into triggers you haven't yet recognized in yourself.

It's tempting to regard some forms of stress as inherent to certain job roles or industries and to accept them as unavoidable. Yet acknowledging your stress triggers isn't about resigning yourself to them; it's about identifying areas where you can exert control or implement changes. Perhaps it's advocating for clearer communication, altering workflows, or setting more realistic expectations with your colleagues and supervisors.

Stress can also arise when your values are misaligned with your organization's practices or mission. Reflecting on your core values is essential. What deeply matters to you, and how well does your work environment reflect that? Such reflections can lead to significant realizations about why certain aspects of your job may cause persistent stress that needs to be addressed.

Technology can be a source of stress as well, from relentless notifications to the allure of always being 'on.'

Evaluate how your digital habits contribute to your stress. Are you incessantly checking emails outside of work hours? Do the pings of incoming messages instantly heighten your anxiety? Setting boundaries with technology—such as scheduled times to check emails or turning off notifications—can mitigate this digital stress.

Life outside of work, too, affects your stress levels within it. Challenges in your personal life don't remain neatly compartmentalized but bleed over into your professional realm. Ensure that you're not overlooking these external factors when attempting to understand the stress you experience at work.

Let's not forget about physical triggers like lack of sleep, poor diet, and insufficient exercise—all of these can magnify work-related stress. Taking care of your body can significantly bolster your resilience against stress. It's crucial to view your health as the foundation upon which your work satisfaction is built.

Once you've recognized your stress triggers, you're in a better position to anticipate and prepare for them. Whether it means altering your behavior, changing how you think about work, or making practical changes to your work environment, you now hold the roadmap to less stressful days ahead.

It's a journey, not a destination. Recognizing your stress triggers is an ongoing process that will evolve along with your career and life. Remaining agile and reflective ensures that as new stressors arise, you're ready to identify and manage them with the toolkit of strategies you're continually developing.

In the following chapters, we'll build upon this foundation of recognition and explore robust strategies for managing these triggers. The power of positive self-talk, setting appropriate boundaries, and other proactive measures can help convert your newfound awareness into real, tangible changes in your work life, setting you on the path toward a happier, healthier professional experience.

The Role of Perception in Work Stress Perception is not just a lens through which we view reality; it's the architect of our experience, especially when it comes to stress in the workplace. We often don't realize how significantly our interpretation of events, demands, and interactions shape our stress levels. Perception is powerful yet malleable, and understanding its role can be transformative.

Consider the element of control—or our perception of it. When we believe we have a handle on our work, even amidst challenges, stress often feels manageable. The converse is also true. If we perceive our work as a chaotic ensemble of tasks we can't control, stress surges. Our mind's interpretation acts as a valve, either releasing or increasing pressure based on our perceived level of control.

But why is this perception so central? It's our internal narrative that dictates how we process experiences. A deadline can be seen as a looming threat or a challenging opportunity, depending upon our mindset. Given the same circumstances, two individuals can experience vastly differing degrees of stress. One person might perceive the deadline as a chance to prove their abilities and grow, while another might see it as a confirmation of their inadequacy.

Our perception of support within the workplace also plays a substantial role in stress. When we feel supported by colleagues, supervisors, and the organization, challenges seem more surmountable. There's a cushioning effect that buffers us from the impact of stress. If, however, we feel isolated or undermined, the same stressful situation can seem insurmountable.

When it comes to feedback—positive or constructive—our perception can either trigger a stress response or reinforce our sense of capability. If we view constructive criticism as an attack rather than a tool for growth, we may experience unnecessary stress. Conversely, when we perceive such feedback as valuable, stress is mitigated, and learning takes place.

What about external stressors? Even these are subject to the filters of perception. A heavy workload might be interpreted as trust in our abilities or as a burdensome expectation. Likewise, organizational changes can be perceived as threats to security or as avenues for professional development.

Perceptions are shaped by past experiences, personal values, and deeply ingrained beliefs. This subjectivity means that altering perception isn't merely a matter of flipping a switch. It's about reframing our interpretation of events, which is a learned skill that calls for patience and practice.

One might ask, how do we adjust our perception? It starts by stepping back and assessing our automatic thoughts. Are they grounded in reality or born from a place of fear and insecurity? By identifying our cognitive distortions, we can begin to dismantle the frameworks that amplify stress.

Mindfulness practices ground us in the present moment, away from catastrophic projections about the future or regrets over the past. This focus aids in cultivating a more balanced perception, one that's aligned with the here and now. In this state of awareness, stressors are stripped down to their facts, minus the embellishment of our anxious minds.

Developing empathy towards ourselves and others is another key strategy in managing perception. Approaching our work with self-compassion when we're struggling can shift our view from one of failure to one of learning. Furthermore, understanding the perspectives and challenges of our colleagues can reduce the stress born from misinterpretations and assumptions.

Let's not forget about the power of open communication. It lifts the veil of assumption by clarifying intent and expectations. When we engage in honest dialogue with our peers and superiors, our perception aligns more closely with reality, easing the ambiguities that can cause stress.

Another angle to consider is the framing effect. The way information is presented to us—whether it's a task description or performance review—can significantly influence our perception. Positive framing by employers can reduce the perception of stress by highlighting potential benefits and learning opportunities embedded in challenging tasks.

Ultimately, recognizing the impermanence of situations can also alleviate stress. Our professional landscape is in a constant state of flux, and our roles within it are no different. Embracing this transitory nature allows us to perceive stressful situations as temporary, and therefore, more bearable.

The cultivation of gratitude plays an oft-underestimated role in shaping perception. When you consciously identify elements of your job that you're grateful for, it can shift the mental spotlight away from stress and towards appreciation. This holistic view powers balance and resilience.

Last but not least, it is crucial to build a toolkit of coping strategies. This personalized collection might include reflective practices, physical activities, or creative outlets. These strategies offer us alternative perspectives, making it easier to perceive stressful situations with clarity and calm.

In the tapestry of workplace wellness, the threads of perception weave prominently throughout. Grasping its pivotal role in stress enables us to navigate our work environments with empowerment and composure, crafting an experience defined not by what happens to us, but by how we choose to perceive it.

Chapter 2: Strategies to Cope with Overwhelming Feelings

Embarking on our journey through the tumultuous sea of work-related stress, we find ourselves confronted with waves of overwhelming feelings. These feelings, if left unchecked, can capsize our well-being and hinder our performance. The key to navigating these choppy waters is to arm ourselves with an arsenal of strategies that can restore calm and clarity.

At the heart of coping is the acknowledgment that our feelings are valid; they are indicators of our state of mind in response to our environment. In a professional setting, feelings of being overwhelmed can arise from myriad sources—tight deadlines, challenging projects, or even interpersonal dynamics. Our task is to recognize these emotions without allowing them to steer the ship.

A fundamental technique for regaining command in moments of high stress is breath control. The simple, yet effective practice of focused breathing serves as an anchor, bringing us back to the present and diffusing immediate tension. Through deep, measured breaths, we directly communicate to our nervous system a signal to ease and relax.

Integrating mindfulness practices into our daily work routine can significantly reduce the magnitude of stress we experience. Mindfulness encourages us to observe our thoughts and feelings without judgment. In doing so, we often discover that our overwhelming feelings dissipate when we give them space to be examined rather than reacted to impulsively.

Positive self-talk is another potent tool in your coping toolkit. The narrative we silently tell ourselves about our abilities and worth has a profound effect on our emotional state. When faced with stress, negotiating with internal critics by reframing thoughts from 'I can't handle this' to 'I'm learning to manage this effectively' can make all the difference.

One of the most empowering actions we can take is setting clear boundaries. It's easy to overcommit in a culture that often equates busyness with productivity. The art of saying 'no' or 'not now' is critical in preserving our energy and maintaining focus on what truly matters at work.

Equally important is creating a sanctuary of time for ourselves. Whether this is through short, scheduled breaks throughout the workday or designated downtime at home, finding moments of solitude allows our thoughts and emotions to settle. By regularly creating a quiet space for reflection, we also nurture our resilience to future stressful situations.

Another strategy often overlooked is the power of a strong support network. Sharing our experiences with trusted colleagues or friends can provide fresh perspectives and strategies. Many times, they have navigated similar challenges and can offer empathy and advice. Feeling understood and supported can dramatically reduce feelings of isolation and stress.

Maintaining a healthy lifestyle as part of our coping strategy cannot be overstated. Regular exercise, a balanced diet, and adequate sleep contribute significantly to our emotional fortitude. When our body is well-cared for, it's better equipped to handle psychological stress.

In our pursuit of balance, periodically unplugging from technology is beneficial. The persistent bombardment of emails, messages, and notifications can lead to information overload. By consciously disconnecting, we grant ourselves a reprieve—a chance to recharge and approach our tasks with renewed energy.

Engaging in creative or leisure activities can also serve as an effective counterbalance to work stress. Whether it's painting, gardening, or playing an instrument, these activities offer an outlet for expression and an opportunity to experience flow—a state where we become fully immersed and lose track of time.

Finally, reflection is a key aspect of coping. Taking time to review what's working and what's not in our approach to stress management ensures that our strategies remain effective. Being open to adjusting our habits means we stay responsive to our needs and the ever-changing demands of the workplace.

As we close this chapter, it's essential to remember that while stress at work is inevitable, succumbing to it is not. By building and practicing a robust set of strategies to cope with overwhelming feelings, we stand firm against the tide. With patience and perseverance, not only can we navigate these waters, but we can also sail forward into calmer, more fulfilling seas of professional life.

Certainly, the subsequent chapters will delve deeper into specific techniques and practices to address work stress comprehensively. But for now, armed with the strategies outlined here, we have a solid foundation to face the emotional challenges that arise from our endeavors in the workplace.

Let us harness these strategies as we continue our quest for happiness at work, productivity, stress management, and the elusive yet attainable work-life balance that fuels our well-being and success.

Breathing Techniques and Mindfulness

In chapter one, we explored the anatomy of work stress and identified personal triggers. Understanding the underpinnings of stress is one thing, but finding tangible methods to alleviate it is quite another. Here, we delve into the world of breathing techniques and mindfulness, keystones in the foundation for stress management and overall well-being.

Breathing, the most vital of human functions, can be a potent ally in calming the mind and body. When under stress, people tend to take shallow breaths which exacerbates feelings of anxiety. On the contrary, deep breathing stimulates the parasympathetic nervous system, which invokes a sense of peace. For instance, the '4-7-8' technique involves inhaling quietly through the nose for a count of four, holding the breath for a count of seven, and exhaling completely through the mouth for a count of eight. This pattern, when repeated three to four times, can be a quick and effective way to reduce tension.

Moving beyond specific patterns, the simple act of becoming mindful of your breathing is in itself a powerful exercise. Mindful breathing, which can be done at any time and place, involves tuning into the rhythm of your breath and taking notice of how it feels in the moment. This form of mindfulness practice promotes an attentive and non-judgmental awareness which helps shift your focus away from stress-laden thoughts.

Guided visualization complements breathing exercises and serves as a catalyst for relaxation. Imagine a serene environment, perhaps a gently flowing river or a quiet forest glade. As you focus on the details of this mental image, synchronize your breathing with the peaceful rhythm of the scene. This mental escape can provide a much-needed break from the stressors of the workplace.

Another facet of mindfulness is the practice of body scanning. Starting from the toes and moving upwards, pay attention to each part of the body, acknowledging any discomfort, tension, or relaxation. This increases bodily awareness, grounding you in the present moment and often leading to a spontaneous release of tension.

Yoga, often considered a physical exercise, is rich in practices that blend breath control with movement and mindfulness. Integrating simple yoga stretches into your daily routine can improve flexibility and also serve as additional opportunities to practice mindful breathing.

As distractions mount, so does the penchant for one's mind to wander. Mindfulness meditation is the art of bringing back the wandering mind to a point of focus, such as the breath, a sound, or a visualization. Performed regularly, it can enhance your ability to remain present and engaged, even amidst a busy work environment.

Progressive muscle relaxation is yet another technique that can dovetail seamlessly with deep breathing. It involves tensing up individual muscle groups as you inhale and releasing them as you exhale, creating a wave of relaxation throughout your body. It's particularly useful after long periods of sitting or during stressful moments when physical tension accumulates.

The concept of 'mindful eating' encourages being fully present with the experience of eating, savoring each bite, and acknowledging colors, textures, and flavors. This not only makes meal times more enjoyable but can also prevent overeating and enhance digestion, which stress can often disrupt.

Mindfulness can weave its way into daily actions and interactions. For example, practicing active listening during conversations can foster a deeper connection with colleagues and clients, reducing misunderstandings and creating a more congenial work environment.

It's important not to underestimate the power of short mindfulness pauses known as 'micro-breaks.' Even a minute taken to focus on your breath or surroundings can act as a reset button, diminishing the cumulative effect of stress and enhancing cognitive function.

The road to embracing mindfulness and integrating breathing techniques into your workday isn't relegated to pre-set durations or locations. The versatility of mindfulness means it can be adapted to fit any schedule or environment - whether it's a two-minute breathing break or a 20-minute meditation session during your commute.

Consistency is key. Integrating breathing techniques and mindfulness into daily routines may not offer immediate gratification, but like any skill, with regular practice, its benefits multiply and over time can lead to greater emotional resilience and a more satisfying work experience.

Understanding these principles and practices forms the bedrock of a happier, more productive work life. Combining mindfulness with deep breathing isn't just a stress-relief technique; it's a way of living that can transform your workday from a flurry of stress into a more controlled, enjoyable experience. So, as we press forward, let's keep these tools in ready reach, and watch as they reshape our engagement with the work environment and beyond.

The following chapters build upon the foundation laid here, offering further strategies to maintain motivation, reduce stress, and improve interpersonal relationships at work. As we proceed, we will see how these principles interlace with other areas to enhance overall work life balance.

The Power of Positive Self-Talk Through the victories and challenges in our professional journeys, the manner in which we converse with ourselves plays a pivotal role in shaping our experiences and outcomes. Engaging in positive self-talk is akin to having an encouraging coach by your side—one that can steer you toward resilience and happiness in your career.

Positive self-talk isn't simply about repeating platitudes or denying negative experiences; it's a robust strategy that, when practiced, can fundamentally alter our brain's pathways, leading to heightened well-being and productivity. The emphasis is on nurturing a compassionate and motivational inner dialogue that moves us toward our objectives and aligns us with our aspirations.

The essence of this technique lies in recognizing the patterns of our internal monologue. Frequently, we may not even be aware that a harsh critic resides within us, sabotaging our confidence with every small misstep. However, by tuning into our thoughts and gently reshaping them from critical to supportive, we can cultivate a more benevolent inner voice—a voice that champions our efforts and soothes us during tumultuous times.

Imagine preparing for a significant presentation. The difference between thinking "I'm not cut out for this" and "I've prepared and can handle whatever comes my way" is profound. One mindset predicts defeat, while the other anticipates success. Adopting a mindset of the latter variety primes us for performance, and even if things don't proceed flawlessly, it fosters a sense of pride in our attempt and resilience.

Positive self-talk also influences stress levels directly. By affirming our capacity to manage and overcome difficulties, we can mitigate the physiological responses associated with stress. Over time, if we consistently feed our mind with affirmative messages, we diminish the production of stress hormones, allowing us to remain calmer and more composed in the face of challenges.

Embracing a positive narrative is not about shunning reality but rather about choosing a perspective that empowers rather than paralyzes. Yes, the workload may be substantial, and yes, there could be difficult coworkers or demanding projects, but by confronting these elements with an attitude of "I have the skills necessary to navigate this" or "I can seek assistance to overcome this obstacle," we place ourselves in a position of control and influence.

The adoption of positive self-talk as a habitual practice may take time. It's essential to be patient with oneself and to recognize that old habits, especially those as deeply ingrained as our thought patterns, do not change overnight. You may choose to use affirmation cards, journaling, or even set reminders to pause for a moment of self-reflection and intentional positivity throughout your day.

Moreover, fostering an attitude of gratitude can significantly amplify the effects of positive self-talk. By routinely acknowledging what we're thankful for in our professional lives—be it supportive colleagues, personal growth opportunities, or successfully completed projects—we augment our positive inner dialogue with a sense of appreciation and fulfillment.

Another integral aspect of positive self-talk is learning to handle failure constructively. Instead of self-reproach, we can guide ourselves to view setbacks as invaluable learning experiences. Reframing failure as feedback not only reduces stress but also metamorphoses our work environment into a learning-rich landscape teeming with opportunities for personal and professional development.

Let's not overlook the contagious nature of positivity. As we develop more positive self-talk habits, the benefits extend beyond our well-being; they can subtly influence the mood and attitudes of those we interact with at the workplace. This affords an atmosphere conducive to collaboration, innovation, and shared success, pivoting the entire work culture towards a more supportive and optimistic direction.

Of course, positive self-talk is but one tool in our toolkit for managing work stress. It compliments other practices such as setting boundaries, mindfulness, and taking regular breaks, all of which collectively contribute to a more harmonious work-life balance. When these various elements integrate seamlessly, we stand to experience significant strides towards our holistic well-being.

The act of instilling positive self-talk into our daily work routine is an investment in our mental health, work satisfaction, and overall productivity. With every positive affirmation, we strengthen our intrinsic belief in our capabilities and worth, equipping ourselves to tackle the ebb and flow of work stress with grace and fortitude.

Keep in mind, this process necessitates a level of self-awareness that allows us to intercept negative thought patterns and replace them with nurturing, affirmative beliefs. The journey towards integrating positive self-talk may demand effort and reflection, yet the dividends it pays in heightened happiness and reduced stress are immeasurable.

So as we navigate our workdays, let's acknowledge the power that our internal discourse holds and pledge to mold it into a force for good—a force that uplifts, encourages, and paves the way to a well-balanced and satisfying professional life.

Setting Boundaries to Preserve Your Energy As we explore the landscape of workplace wellness, an essential phenomenon often overlooked is the art of setting boundaries to preserve one's energy. Imagine for a moment a garden with all sorts of radiant flowers, vibrant greens, and titillating scents. This garden thrives because of its defined boundaries that protect it from trampling feet and invasive species. Similarly, at work, our personal boundaries shield our mental and emotional well-being, enabling us to flourish.

Boundaries at work are not barriers to engagement or productivity. On the contrary, they serve as the framework within which we can operate at our peak. Think of boundaries as a personal policy that dictates how others can interact with us, what tasks we take on, and how we allocate our time. They enable us to say 'yes' to what truly matters and 'no' to what drains us.

Establishing clear boundaries starts by identifying what we value most. Is it quality time with family? Is it our health and personal development? Or is it dedicated periods for deep work? Understanding our values helps us pinpoint where we need to draw lines. For example, a boundary may look like not checking emails after 6 PM to ensure quality family time or not eating lunch at your desk to allow a mental break from work tasks.

Let's not mistake a boundary for rigidity. Boundaries aren't static; we must negotiate them with the fluidity of our workday. Yet, they require assertiveness—a kind inner strength that empowers us to respectfully express our limits without fear of being perceived as uncooperative. Assertiveness is not aggressiveness; it is simply claiming the space for oneself with dignity and respect for others.

Communication is the vehicle through which we establish boundaries. It must be clear, consistent, and structured in a way that leaves little room for misunderstandings. For instance, if working late hours is becoming habitual and affecting your health, have a candid discussion with your manager about restructuring your workload.

When setting boundaries, anticipate some pushback or testing from colleagues and management. It's human nature to resist change, and boundaries can be seen as change. Stay firm and remember your boundaries are there to preserve the most important asset you have—your energy and well-being.

It is also of paramount importance to establish technology boundaries. The digital age has blurred the lines between work and home life. To maintain energy reserves, it might be necessary to silence notifications, schedule specific slots to check emails, and even take a deliberate hiatus from digital devices during non-work hours.

Remember, self-care is not self-indulgence. Self-care actions like stepping away from your desk regularly may seem small, but they have a compound effect on energy preservation. These actions are part of the boundaries that create a sustainable work rhythm.

Boundaries must also extend to interpersonal relationships at work. Learning how to navigate small talk, avoid gossip, and not get entangled in draining emotional dramas with coworkers protects your mental space. Engage with empathy and kindness, but do not let the emotional states of others overshadow your own.

Delegation is a boundary strategy. By handing off tasks that can be completed by others, you reserve your energy for tasks that require your expertise. This doesn't mean neglecting responsibilities—it means intelligently managing your work portfolio to avoid overload and burnout.

Fostering boundaries also includes saying no to additional assignments when your plate is full. It's all too easy to take on more than we can handle in an effort to seem indispensable. However, when we overcommit, our work quality and energy levels plummet. Learn the skill of politely declining or negotiating deadlines that allow for high-quality output without depleting your reserves.

Personal boundaries are reinforced by professional boundaries. This means respecting the working hours, recognizing the limits of our job descriptions, and not feeling compelled to carry the weight of responsibilities that aren't ours to bear.

Sustaining boundaries is a practice you cultivate daily. It requires self-awareness, self-respect, and the understanding that you're the steward of your own energy. Check in with yourself often. Are your boundaries still serving you? Are they being respected? Make adjustments as necessary, keeping your well-being at the forefront.

Setting boundaries at work is not just a remedy for stress—it's a proactive step towards crafting a career and a life that's sustainable and rewarding. When we're honest about our limits, when we're brave enough to maintain them, and when we communicate them with grace, we set the stage for a workplace experience that is meaningful and invigorating.

As we close this section, we walk away with a newfound appreciation for boundaries. They are not walls that keep others out, but rather the thresholds that invite our best selves in. By honoring our personal limits, we give ourselves the permission to thrive not just professionally, but holistically. So, let's carry forward this understanding and implement boundaries with clarity and conviction, for our energy is too precious a resource to squander.

Chapter 3:
Achieving Focus Amidst Distractions

In an age where notification pings are continuous, and the allure of multitasking is ever-present, achieving true focus at work can seem like a herculean task. However, the tranquility of a focused mind is not only attainable, but it is also vital for our productivity and overall wellbeing. The journey to overcoming the incessant babbles of distractions begins with strategic inner adjustments and an intentional approach towards the outer environment.

The key to honing one's focus lies in understanding the nature and impact of interruptions that plague the modern workplace. Smartphones, social media alerts, and the infinite scroll of information can fracture our attention, making it challenging to engage deeply with our work. To counteract this, we must cultivate a mindset that embraces concentration as a skill to be developed, much like a muscle that gains strength with consistent training.

Rise Above

Establishing a clear sense of priority forms the cornerstone of effective focus. When we engage in the act of prioritizing, we grant ourselves the permission to concentrate on what truly matters, stage by stage. It's not merely identifying the most critical tasks; it's a commitment to honoring the choices made, allowing for a seamless immersion in the task at hand, free from the guilt of neglecting lesser tasks.

Within this ballet of concentration, mono-tasking emerges as a quiet revolution against the myth of multitasking. There's magic in mono-tasking, a serene profundity in experiencing one task as if it's the only task that exists at that moment. This doesn't mean that other tasks are forgotten, but they are respectfully queued, awaiting their turn for undivided attention.

Our workspaces, be they at home or in a bustling office, can transform into sanctuaries of focus when tailored to limit external distractions. It might involve physical tweaks, like noise-cancelling headphones, or creating subtle rituals that signal to our minds that it's time to delve deep. The ambience of our physical environment can nurture a focal mindset, one where clarity flourishes and distractions dissolve.

Yet, shifting the atmosphere and habits may not suffice. Sometimes, it's the internal chatter that we must address. The gentle art of guiding our thoughts back to the present task, without chastising our wandering minds, can be a gentle nudge towards sustained focus. It requires patience and an understanding that the mind, curious by nature, may occasionally stray. The mastery is not in chaining it down, but in guiding it back, softly but resolutely.

For some, the encroachment of digital barrages is not easily brushed aside. Applications designed to filter the unnecessary and highlight the essential can be allies in our quest to preserve mental real estate for the work that makes a difference. A digital detox, periodically unplugging from the matrix of ceaseless connectivity, can rejuvenate our ability to concentrate when we return to our digital domain.

A mention on the significance of strategic breaks should not go unheard. At regular intervals, stepping away from work to take a brisk walk or to simply gaze outside can reset our mental state. It's in these moments of repose that our subconscious mind often pieces together the scattered fragments of an earlier focus, gifting us insights upon our return to work.

It's also about recognizing that our days are an ebb and flow of energy and attention. There will be times when focus comes easily and other times when it feels just beyond our reach. This isn't failure; it's the rhythm of human productivity. Learning our own cadence and planning our most demanding tasks accordingly can heighten our efficiency and ease the strain we often put on ourselves to perform consistently.

Last but not least, granting ourselves grace as we strive for focus in a world of distractions is essential. It's not about achieving perfection in our concentration; it's about understanding our human tendencies and developing strategies to gently align our attention with our intentions. By doing so, we weave tranquility into our work lives, bolstering our happiness, productivity, and balance amid the ever-present whirlwind of the world around us.

Prioritization: Tackling the Most Critical Tasks First

Embarking on the journey to manage work stress and maintain happiness and productivity, it's instrumental to engage with our tasks intentionally. As you focus on achieving focus amidst the plethora of workplace distractions, the essence of prioritization cannot be overstated. It's about excelling at not just doing things right, but doing the right things.

Understanding what is essential and what can wait plays a pivotal role in not only how much you achieve but also in the satisfaction you derive from your work. Our cognition is fine-tuned to sense fulfillment when we tackle meaningful tasks, which requires discernment and a robust approach to prioritize successfully.

Begin by assessing the scope of your responsibilities with a critical eye. Every task demands scrutiny to determine its impact on the broader canvas of your goals. Evaluate which tasks have the highest payoff in terms of value, whether through advancing career objectives, contributing to team success, or aligning with personal fulfillment. Thoughtful consideration can illuminate which tasks are merely urgent versus those that are truly important.

Once you've identified the most critical tasks, give yourself the permission to focus. This is the cornerstone of effective prioritization—one must concentrate all their energies on the task that promises the highest yields. It's often tempting to opt for low-hanging fruit, accomplishing simpler tasks for a quick sense of achievement. However, dedicating your prime time to critical tasks can lead to significant progress.

Planning is your ally here. Start each day with a plan that not only lists your tasks but ranks them in order of importance. This doesn't necessarily mean that the most challenging tasks should always come first, but rather those with deadlines and the greatest significance should be front and center. Allow flexibility in your plan to accommodate the unpredictable nature of work life. Understand that sometimes, priorities shift, and adaptability is key.

Setting realistic expectations for what can be achieved in a given timeframe is also part of prioritizing. Even the most industrious among us can't perform miracles. Acknowledge that ticking off every item on a to-do list is not always feasible and focus your efforts where they count the most. Such acceptance doesn't signify a lowering of standards, but rather a strategic allocation of time and resources.

In the vein of tackling critical tasks first, acknowledge that human energy is limited. It waxes and wanes during the day. Knowing when you are at your peak performance level allows you to align these periods with your most demanding tasks. There's wisdom in aligning complexity with capability.

Implementing a system to manage tasks can further enhance your prioritization efforts. Whether it's a digital tool or a physical planner, find a system that resonates with you and stick with it. A visible reminder of your priorities helps keep your focus sharp and your commitment to them strong. Checking off completed tasks isn't just practical; it also provides a psychological boost.

There are inherent lessons in the act of prioritizing that go beyond immediate task management. It's a lesson in values, in understanding what truly matters to you and why. Through prioritization, you learn more about yourself—your capacity for work, your values, your aspirations. This self-awareness is crucial as it underpins your entire approach to work and life balance.

Moreover, prioritizing critical tasks is also an exercise in saying no. Opportunities and demands will come your way, but not all will be conducive to reaching your objectives. Being able to turn down requests that don't align with your key tasks is a form of self-preservation and focus. It's not about being uncooperative, but rather about being strategically cooperative.

The principles of prioritization can ripple into teamwork as well. Sharing your approach with colleagues and understanding their priorities can create a symphony of focused effort, where everyone's energy is aligned and directed towards collective goals. Teamwork is heightened when all members know what their key contributions should be.

Remember, prioritization is a constant process, not a one-time arrangement. Regularly revisiting and adjusting your priorities keeps them relevant and effective. With the fast-paced nature of many workplaces, what was important one week may be overtaken by new developments the next. Stay dynamic in your prioritization to remain at the forefront of productivity.

Let's not forget that while work is a significant part of life, it's not the entirety. Prioritize tasks at work by all means, but also prioritize life outside of work. This balance ensures that while you excel professionally, you also thrive personally. A holistic approach to prioritization leads to a rich and fulfilling life, both at the office and beyond.

Ultimately, the art of prioritizing is deeply personal and exceptionally powerful. It's the strategic cornerstone that allows you to build a career and a life that is both productive and joyful. Embrace prioritization as a pathway to excellence, a skill that bolsters your ability to make a meaningful impact. Let this not just be a tool, but a guiding philosophy for a rewarding and balanced existence.

The Magic of Mono-tasking

In a world that constantly heralds multitasking as the pinnacle of productivity, there lies a hidden gem that quietly boosts efficiency and preserves our mental well-being: mono-tasking. The concept, simple yet profound, involves dedicating one's undivided attention to a single task at a time. Its beauty lies in the rich engagement and focused energy it fosters, allowing for a deeper immersion in the work at hand.

To grasp the magic of mono-tasking, imagine a day where each task, like pearls on a string, is given its moment to shine without the distraction of other gems vying for attention. It's in this mindful approach to work that a sense of calm clarity can emerge. When you dive wholeheartedly into a piece of work, you cultivate not only productivity but also a mental space where stress struggles to take root.

Why is mono-tasking so powerful? Science suggests that when we attempt to juggle multiple tasks, our brains engage in constant context switching. This switch is not as seamless as one might imagine. It comes with a cognitive cost, much like a tax on your brain's efficiency. Mono-tasking, on the other hand, allows the brain to settle into a single endeavor, reducing mental fatigue and errors.

Let's take a step further into the practical applications of this approach. When planning your day, identify the task that, once completed, will give you the highest sense of accomplishment. This pivotal task then becomes the focus of a mono-tasking session. By clearing away other potential distractions, you give this task the full breadth of your intellectual and creative power.

As you implement mono-tasking, anticipate initial resistance. Our brains have been trained to crave the dopamine hits that come with new emails, social media notifications, and the illusion of productivity that multitasking brings. Learning to resist this urge is much like building muscle; it takes consistent effort and the results are gradually realized.

In practice, mono-tasking can look different for everyone. For some, it's working in quiet solitude; for others, it's the gentle hum of a coffee shop that fosters singular focus. It's essential to find the environment that best supports your mono-tasking efforts.

The role of technology, often a distractor, can be reconfigured to support your mono-tasking endeavors. Use tools that block out noise and shut off notifications during dedicated work times. Digital tools, when used intentionally, can create a protective barrier around your focused work time.

Mono-tasking also offers an antidote to the incessant busyness that plagues the modern work culture. It's an invitation to slow down, to do less but to do it better. Quality, in the mono-tasking philosophy, trumps quantity because deep work leads to profound outcomes – outcomes that are often diluted in the sea of multitasking madness.

It's worth noting that the mastery of mono-tasking doesn't happen overnight. Just as it is with any skill worth cultivating, it arrives through patient and persistent practice. Starting small, with short mono-tasking blocks, and gradually expanding them as your focus muscle strengthens, can ease you into a more sustained mono-tasking practice.

One of the most compelling benefits of mono-tasking is the space it creates for innovation and creativity. Problem-solving flourishes in an environment where thoughts aren't fragmented. Ideas have room to breathe and grow, and this is where creativity finds its wings.

Another unspoken beauty of mono-tasking is the state it can invoke, often referred to as flow. This state, characterized by complete absorption in a task, not only heightens enjoyment but often leads to peak performance. It's in this state that we frequently find true fulfillment in our work.

Moreover, mono-tasking aligns with the philosophy of presence. When focused on the task at hand, there is a heightened sense of being truly present in the moment. This mindfulness aspect not only improves the quality of your work but also enriches the overall experience of your day, reducing feelings of being overwhelmed.

Those who embrace mono-tasking often discover improved communication in the workplace. With their minds not splintered among various tasks, they listen more actively and engage more thoughtfully. This can lead to stronger, more meaningful professional relationships.

The magic of mono-tasking lies not only in its ability to increase productivity but equally in its capacity to enhance mental well-being and job satisfaction. As you peel away the layers of multitasking's allure and settle into the rhythm of mono-tasking, you may find that your work becomes a source of joy rather than stress, and your ability to balance the demands of work and life improves immeasurably.

As we close this section, let us carry with us the notion that in the art of work, it's not always the quantity of tasks completed that measures success. Sometimes, it is the depth of engagement, the quality of execution, and the ability to find joy and purpose in the work we do. Monotasking paves the way towards such a fulfilling work experience, one meticulously crafted task at a time.

Creating a Distraction-Free Workspace In the quest for achieving focus amidst the barrage of daily distractions, the design of one's workspace is not merely a backdrop; it's an active participant in the theater of productivity. Envisioning a personal haven where distractions are but a distant murmur requires intention and strategy.

Consider the physical realm of your workspace. Clutter, that insidious accumulator of chaos, can all too easily impede your mental clarity. Begin by reclaiming your territory, one where each item serves a purpose and excess is diligently banished. A minimalist approach not only soothes the eye but also streamlines the decision-making process about what to tackle next.

The often overlooked element of lighting plays a pivotal role in crafting a conducive work environment. Position your desk to take advantage of natural light, cultivating an ambiance that energizes and sharpens focus. On cloudier days or during late hours, ensure your artificial lighting is ample and gentle on the eyes, avoiding the harshness that could lead to fatigue.

Soundscapes can be as distracting as tangibles. If your workspace can't be insulated against the commotion of the outside world, consider noise-cancelling headphones or soft background music that can mask interruptions. The aim is not silence but the creation of a consistent auditory environment where unexpected noises don't break your stride.

Your chair, the throne from which you command your empire of tasks, should be a paragon of ergonomic support. Spare no effort in selecting a chair that cradles you comfortably for the hours you'll spend seated. Physical discomfort is a surefire way to fracture concentration and invite musculoskeletal stress.

Location is another contender in the ring of focus. If possible, stake out a spot that is designated for work alone. By creating a clear separation between work and leisure areas, you foster a psychological trigger that signals to your mind it's time to hone in on tasks the moment you settle into your work zone.

Personalization adds a layer of comfort to your workspace while maintaining its status as a productivity sanctuary. Items that signify serenity or motivation to you

– plants, art, or simple keepsakes – can forge an association of positivity and purpose in your work environment.

Technology, a double-edged sword in the modern era, requires conscientious monitoring. Every notification, pop-up, and digital alert is an invitation for your attention to stray. Take control by taming your devices with do-not-disturb modes during peak productivity periods and using website blockers to keep digital wandering at bay.

Consider the air you breathe, and invest in a bit of greenery or an air purifier to ensure your lungs are filled with nothing but the best. Good air quality is subtle but crucial for maintaining alertness and well-being throughout your workday.

Don't underestimate the power of routine in solidifying a distraction-free workspace. Establishing and adhering to specific practices, such as clearing your desk at the end of the day or starting with a calming ritual, can reinforce the sanctity of your workspace.

When the workspace is shared with others, boundaries must be communicated and respected. This might involve setting clear guidelines about interruptions, wearing headphones, or even visual indicators (like a small flag) that signal when you're in deep focus mode and should not be disturbed.

Managing cables and technological clutter is another step in retaining a clear mind. Opt for wireless options where feasible, use cable organizers to keep everything in its place, and ensure your work-tech is supportive, not invasive, of your work process.

Temperature control can't be ignored if you're looking to fashion a distraction-free zone. Being too cold or too hot can pull your focus away faster than a siren's song. Aim for a comfortable temperature range where you can work without noticing the air around you – a seamless environment that supports your workflow.

Refreshments should not be an ordeal requiring a journey. Have a water bottle at hand and snack options within reach so that sustenance doesn't become a distraction in itself. A small, dedicated space for hydration and nutrition keeps you fueled without pulling you away from your objectives for long.

Spend time at the end of each day to review how your space functioned. Was there a recurrent distraction that can be mitigated? Is there an adjustment that could enhance your focus? Continuous refinement of your environment not only keeps it aligned with your evolving needs but also reinforces your commitment to fostering productivity.

By tailoring every facet of your workspace to anchor you in the flow of work, you sculpt not just a physical location but a mindset. A distraction-free workspace is a crucible within which the chemistry of productivity is made possible, where focus is the rule and not the exception, allowing you to achieve an equilibrium of happiness, productivity, stress management, and work-life balance.

Chapter 4: Mastering Your To-Do List

As we journey further into mastering workplace well-being, it's essential to confront the ever-present to-do list—a relentless reminder of our commitments and tasks. A well-structured to-do list can be a powerful ally, transforming chaotic workloads into manageable units. It's all about finding harmony within the list, making use of it as a tool rather than allowing it to become a master. Begin by accepting that while a list may represent aspirations of productivity, its true value lies in its ability to guide you efficiently through the workday, ensuring nothing essential falls through the cracks.

The secret to an empowering to-do list is the art of breaking down large tasks into smaller, digestible components. It's easy to feel overwhelmed when a project appears gargantuan, but by dissecting it into actionable steps, progress becomes achievable. There's a tactile satisfaction in ticking off these miniature milestones that accumulates into a sense of substantial progress. This act does more than move a project forward—it elevates mood and nourishes the inner drive that propels you through the workday.

Fine-tuning the to-do list isn't merely a solo act; it's also about discerning when and what to delegate. The art of delegation is not about offloading work to lighten your load; it's a strategic dance of empowering others, creating collaborative synergy, and optimizing team skills. Mastering your to-do list is much like orchestrating a symphony: each instrument has a role, and when played together, they create a harmonious melody of productivity. The ensuing chapters will delve into the intricacies of leveraging technology in task management and embracing delegation, but for now, remember this: the mastery of your to-do list is not in its length, but in its capacity to transform overwhelming noise into a clear, actionable signal.

Breaking Down Large Tasks When faced with a monumental to-do list, it's easy to feel overwhelmed and paralyzed by the sheer volume of work that looms ahead. However, as the saying goes, 'The journey of a thousand miles begins with a single step.' In work as in life, breaking down large tasks into manageable pieces not only makes the tasks appear less daunting, but it also provides a clearer path to completion.

Think of a large task as a puzzle. At first glance, it's nothing more than a jumbled collection of interlocking pieces. However, approach the puzzle piece by piece, starting with separating out the edges, and slowly but surely, the image begins to take shape. Similarly, with a large work task, start by identifying its 'edges'—the defining scope and milestones that mark the progress towards completion.

Set aside time to deconstruct the task at hand. This isn't just busywork; it's a strategic move to gain perspective. Outline the task's components—either on paper or with the use of project management software. Visualization is an essential step, as it allows you to see exactly what you're dealing with, making the task less abstract and more tangible.

Once you've got the big picture laid out, identify the immediate action items. These are the steps you can initiate right away without the need for additional information or prerequisites. By tackling these first, you create positive momentum, which is crucial for motivation and overall productivity.

Understanding that progress is made in layers, take heed not to overextend yourself. Concentrate on one layer at a time. Just like painting a detailed portrait, you wouldn't try to perfect the shadows and highlights before you've sketched the outline. This step-by-step approach naturally prioritizes your efforts and helps maintain focus, ensuring that every hour spent is an hour used effectively.

It's also vital to set interim goals, which serve as checkpoints on your journey. These smaller achievements are opportunities to review and adjust your approach where necessary. Celebrate each of these milestones, reinforcing that sense of accomplishment and renewing your energy to tackle the next phase of the task.

Flexibility in your process is a hidden key to managing large tasks efficiently. Bear in mind that plans may need adaptation when new information comes to light or when external factors shift. Resilience in the face of change ensures that you remain effective and responsive to the evolving nature of work, rather than stuck adhering to an outdated plan.

Incorporate regular assessments of your progress. This isn't simply looking back at what you've done; it's taking a comprehensive view of the road ahead. Are the remaining actions still relevant? Have priorities shifted? This re-evaluation is a powerful tool in keeping your approach fresh and aligned with the end goal.

For instance, if you're working on developing a new product, break down the process into stages such as research, design, prototyping, testing, and launch. As you journey through these stages, maintain communication with stakeholders, collecting feedback and integrating new ideas to refine the product before its final launch.

Delegate tasks whenever possible. You may be capable of executing each step on your own, but it's not always the most efficient use of your time and energy. Recognizing which components can be handed off to capable team members not only lightens your load but also fosters a collaborative atmosphere and helps develop others' skills.

Avoid the trap of perfectionism in the early stages of tackling a project. Striving for excellence is commendable, but perfectionism can lead to procrastination or unnecessary delays. Be willing to push forward with 'good enough' when it meets the requirements, and refine later as needed. Progress often outweighs the allure of perfection.

During the process, it's crucial to maintain balance to prevent burnout. This might mean stepping away from the task for a short period to clear your head or shifting your attention to a different, less intensive task before coming back with renewed focus. Remember that sustained productivity requires both dedication and rest.

Technology can be a double-edged sword, so use it wisely. While apps and digital tools can streamline processes and keep tasks organized, they can also introduce distractions. Choose tools that augment your productivity without overcomplicating the task at hand.

Above all, keep in mind that the essence of work is not just completing tasks but also the growth experienced throughout the process. Breaking down tasks presents opportunities to learn, experiment, and refine your skills. The task may be large, but your capacity for tackling it is even greater when approached with purpose and strategy.

The art of breaking down large tasks lies in understanding the whole, dissecting it into parts, and methodically addressing each segment with focus and flexibility. Maintain clarity of purpose, be open to adaptation, and allow each step forward to build your confidence as you make your way to task completion. Achieving this harmony between effort and strategy is key to happiness and success at work.

Leveraging Technology for Task Management in today's rapidly evolving workplace requires an astute understanding of various tools that can propel one's productivity and ensure a balanced approach to work. It's easy to be overwhelmed with the vast selection of technology options available, each promising to be the solution to our task management woes. However, when chosen judiciously and used effectively, technology can indeed become a powerful ally in managing our daily tasks, reducing stress, and enhancing our overall sense of well-being at work.

To begin, it's important to clarify what technology for task management entails. Essentially, these technologies include applications and software designed to help you organize, prioritize, and automate your tasks. They range from simple to-do list apps to more complex project management tools. Each carries potential benefits that can help you streamline your workday, manage your time more effectively, and maintain focus on your goals.

Digital task management systems allow us to capture tasks as they come to mind, ensuring that nothing falls through the cracks. This is a significant departure from juggling mental lists or scrambling to find paper notes. With a few keystrokes, tasks can be entered, categorized, and even delegated. The resulting clarity can go a long way in reducing the mental load that contributes to work stress.

Furthermore, many of these tools incorporate the concept of 'prioritization'— a foundational skill covered earlier. By enabling users to label tasks according to urgency and importance, technology aids in the efficient organization of one's day. This approach aligns with the principles of tackling the most critical tasks first, thereby ensuring progress in what truly moves the needle.

Another valuable aspect of technology in task management is its ability to promote mono-tasking. Using features such as time-blocking or focused work sessions, professionals can commit dedicated time to individual tasks, minimizing the temptation to multitask. This encourages deeper engagement with the task at hand and can lead to superior quality work and greater personal satisfaction.

Creating a distraction-free workspace is an ongoing challenge in the modern office environment. With notifications continually vying for our attention, task management tools can offer features that help to minimize interruptions. Features such as 'do not disturb' modes or scheduled focus times can help preserve your productivity sanctuary amidst the noise of digital chatter.

The automation of recurring tasks can liberate countless hours previously spent on mundane activities. Whether it's automating email responses, scheduling meetings, or even managing follow-ups, task management technologies can perform these functions with little to no human intervention, allowing you to devote more time to high-value activities.

The integration of various applications through these technologies serves to create a seamless workflow. Task management tools often integrate with email clients, calendars, cloud storage, and other apps, bringing a cohesive experience to managing your workload. This interconnectedness ensures that your task management system acts as a central hub for your day's activities.

Delegation, when done well, can be a significant stress reliever. Some task management tools are designed with team collaboration in mind, making it simple to assign tasks to others and track their progress. This not only enhances team productivity but also broadens the collective capacity to achieve objectives, a critical element as we look towards fostering teamwork and creating a positive workplace culture.

Tracking the progress of tasks not only helps in maintaining accountability but also serves as a motivator. Many technology solutions offer sophisticated reporting and analytics features, making it easy to visualize progress and adjust plans and strategies accordingly. These insights can be a source of motivation, as they provide tangible evidence of small wins along the way.

It's also vital to recognize the role rewards play in sustaining effort and motivation. Modern task management applications often have built-in gamification elements—such as points, badges, and leaderboards—to offer a sense of achievement and recognition that can bolster morale.

Moreover, with technology, the ability to connect work to personal goals becomes more tangible. Many task management tools allow for the setting of personal milestones and professional development targets alongside everyday work tasks. This fusion fosters a more holistic view of productivity—one that encompasses both career aspirations and personal growth.

Stress reduction techniques such as taking breaks and exercise can also be woven into your task management system. For example, reminders to stand up and stretch, or prompts to step away from the desk for a brief walk. These timely cues encourage regular breaks, which are crucial for long-term mental and physical health.

For those advocating for workplace accommodations, the data accumulated within task management tools can provide evidence to support the need for such adjustments. It can highlight times of peak productivity, suggesting flexible work hours, or identify workload imbalances that may necessitate additional resources or support.

It's evident that technology for task management, when leveraged correctly, aligns beautifully with reducing work stress and cultivating a healthy, balanced approach to labor. It acts as a linchpin that connects and reinforces many of the strategies previously discussed, weaving them into the fabric of everyday work life to bolster happiness, productivity, and contentment in the workplace.

As we harness the convenience and efficiency that technology brings to task management, we mustn't lose sight of the ultimate goal: our well-being. Technology serves as our instrument, not our master. With thoughtful integration and mindful utilization, it empowers us to work smarter and live better, thereby enriching not just our career, but every facet of our lives.

The Art of Delegation is an essential skill that, when mastered, can profoundly transform how you approach your to-do list. Delegation is not simply about offloading tasks; it's an intricate dance of trust, communication, and strategic decision-making. It requires a deep understanding of your team's strengths, an appreciation for nuanced task breakdown, and a willingness to let go of the reins to empower others.

Imagine your workday as a symphony. Each instrument and musician plays a vital role, and while you may conduct, you can't play every part. Delegation mirrors this harmonious collaboration, where each team member's individual talents contribute to the collective performance. A conductor who tries to play every instrument will soon find the music is off-key—similarly, attempting to handle every task yourself can lead to a discordant work life and stunted productivity.

To practice effective delegation, you must first identify tasks that are suitable for delegation. These will generally be tasks that are either time-consuming or can be adequately accomplished by someone else. Assess not just the task itself, but also its scope, complexity, and the potential learning opportunities it could provide for the person taking it on.

Once you've earmarked tasks for delegation, choose the right person for the job by aligning the task with their skillset and career aspirations. Just as throwing a novice into the deep-end without support is fruitless, delegating a task to someone without the requisite skills can lead to frustration and poor results. However, when done correctly, it serves as a powerful growth and learning tool for the individual while freeing up your time for high-priority projects.

Successful delegation also depends on your ability to communicate clearly. This means articulating the desired outcome, providing context for the task, setting well-defined parameters, and establishing clear deadlines. Just as clarity in music allows for each note to be heard, clarity in delegation ensures that actions are well-directed and outcomes are harmonious with organizational goals.

Trust is the backbone of delegation. You need to resist the urge to micromanage and instead express confidence in your team's capabilities. Give them the autonomy to approach the task in their own way while remaining available for guidance. As on a trust-building ropes course, you are both the supporter on the ground and the cheerleader from afar, ensuring safety but encouraging independence.

One of the risks of delegation is the fear of diminished quality. To mitigate this, establish checkpoints where you can review progress without encroaching on the autonomy you've granted. Consider these checkpoints as brief intermissions during a musical performance, opportunities to tune the instruments and ensure everything is in harmony before moving forward.

Encourage feedback and dialogue throughout the process. Delegation is not a one-way street; it's a collaborative journey. Open lines of communication allow for real-time adjustments and foster mutual respect. Just as a seasoned conductor listens to their musicians and adjusts accordingly, you must be responsive to your team's input and active in the shared goal of task completion.

It is worth noting that not all tasks can or should be delegated. As a diligent steward of your responsibilities, you'll keep certain high-impact or sensitive tasks in your realm. Just as a conductor holds the baton, some responsibilities must remain firmly in your hand to maintain the integrity and direction of the team's efforts.

Write down information from each delegated task. What worked? What didn't? How can you improve your delegation strategy? This constant refinement is like a musician practicing scales—it's the backbone of improvement that leads to mastery.

Remember, delegation is not a surrender of responsibility but rather a strategic distribution of it. At its core, it's an empowering act that, when performed with skill, can lighten your load, develop your team's abilities, and increase overall productivity.

It's also a commitment to your own well-being. By distributing tasks effectively, you're bolstering your capacity to maintain a harmonious work-life balance. You're giving yourself the breathing room to step back, to innovate, and to approach challenges with a clear mind.

As with all aspects of managing your workload, delegation comes with its own set of challenges. It demands that you balance control with reliance on others, and performance outcomes with individual growth. This can be uncomfortable at first, but with practice, the art of delegation becomes less about losing control and more about gaining collaborative strength.

When successful, the art of delegation results in a shared sense of accomplishment. Just as a standing ovation is for both the conductor and the orchestra, the successful completion of delegated tasks is a collective victory. It is the fruit of trust, clear communication, strategic choice, and shared effort.

Delegating effectively is about embracing a leadership role that is not self-centered but other-embracing, where your success and your team's development are intertwined. Nurturing this skill can lead to a happier, more productive work environment and is integral to achieving the harmony between personal well-being and professional success.

Integrating the art of delegation into your routine will not happen overnight. It is a skill that evolves with experience and intention. With patience and practice, you'll find that delegation is not just a skill for managing tasks – it is an essential component of thriving in the workplace and beyond.

Chapter 5:
Motivation Maintenance

Maintaining motivation in one's professional life is not unlike tending a garden: it requires consistency, the right tools, and a bit of patience. As we move through the thickets of daily work, finding the drive to continue can sometimes feel elusive. Yet, it is this very drive that propels us towards our objectives.

At the heart of motivation lies the notion of momentum—the ability to initiate action and continue moving forward even when hurdles arise. Momentum can be generated through setting and achieving small victories. These minor triumphs are powerful because they create a sense of progress, which fuels further action. Ticking off items on your to-do list or meeting quick turn-around deadlines can give an immediate boost, affirming that you are capable and that the journey, though challenging, is navigable.

However, the pursuit of success isn't just about crossing items off a checklist; it's about sustaining effort over the long haul. This is where understanding the role of rewards comes into play. Encouraging yourself with meaningful rewards after reaching certain milestones can reinvigorate your enthusiasm. These need not be grand gestures but rather something as simple as allowing yourself a favorite treat, a walk in the park, or some other form of personal indulgence that acknowledges your hard work.

Consider, too, the deeper underpinnings of what drives you. Connecting your daily tasks to personal goals and values infuses your work with purpose. This isn't always self-evident, so it requires thoughtful reflection. Ask yourself: How does my work impact others? How does each project align with my personal growth, ethics, or long-term aspirations?

There's something inherently rewarding about feeling part of something larger than oneself. When you can draw a line between the task at hand and a bigger picture, even the most mundane work can gain new meaning. This alignment is the essence of intrinsic motivation—it comes from within and is one of the most durable forms of motivation.

Nonetheless, maintaining motivation isn't merely a solitary endeavor. The environment where you work also plays a crucial role. Surrounding yourself with motivated individuals can have a contagiously positive effect. Just as others' enthusiasm can buoy your spirit, sharing your own progress can inspire those around you, creating a cycle of mutual encouragement.

Adversely, motivation can wane when faced with repetitive tasks that seem to offer little in terms of learning or growth. This is where the art of re-framing your perspective becomes a valuable tool. Even routine duties can be seen as opportunities to refine skills, become more efficient, or even mentor others in these tasks. A shift in outlook can transform a stagnant situation into a developmental stepping stone.

Still, there will be days when the motivation well seems dry despite all efforts. Recognize that fluctuations in drive are a natural part of the human experience. It's not a failing but rather an invitation to re-evaluate and, if necessary, redirect your energy. Reflect on what has changed: Have your goals shifted? Are you feeling burnt out? Are there unaddressed obstacles that need your attention?

This process of continual self-assessment is key to motivation maintenance. Just as no two plants are alike, each individual's motivational needs are unique and may require different nourishment. It could be that taking a break, seeking mentorship, or reshaping objectives is what's needed to invigorate your motivation.

Above all, be patient with yourself. Motivation isn't a constant state; it's more akin to the ebb and flow of tides—responsive to both internal and external forces. Acknowledging this can alleviate the pressure to be in perpetual motion and allow you to harness motivation's natural rhythms.

In the process of maintaining motivation, you are also cultivating resilience. Every effort to push through uncertainty, every attempt to find joy in your work, builds a foundation of strength that will serve you in unpredictable times. Challenges, when faced with a motivated mindset, become not just obstacles but opportunities for growth and learning.

Easing into a state of flow can also amplify your motivation. This occurs when you are fully immersed and engaged in an activity, losing track of time and external pressures. Achieving flow often involves tackling tasks that are challenging yet match your skill level, allowing for a harmonious dance between ability and aspiration.

It's important to celebrate your successes along the way. Taking time to acknowledge and enjoy your accomplishments fortifies your resolve for future endeavors. Whether it's through a reflective journaling session, sharing achievements with friends, or simply taking a moment for quiet gratitude, these practices ground you in your progress and reinforce your motivational foundation.

As we consider motivation maintenance, it becomes clear that it is not solely about individual willpower. It's a multifaceted practice that blends personal introspection, strategic action, supportive environments, and an appreciation for the journey itself. With this holistic approach, you can sustain the vigor that keeps you moving towards your goals with both determination and balance.

We are creatures of habit, pattern, and rhythm. Instilling practices that maintain motivation not only propels us in our current endeavors but also prepares us for future challenges. And as we refine these practices, we don't just work towards happiness and productivity—we're sculpting a lifestyle that embodies them.

Setting and Achieving Small Wins

Embarking on the journey of transforming our work life into a source of joy and accomplishment involves the cultivation of daily victories. The philosophy behind setting and achieving small wins is that success is a compound effect. Small, consistent steps lead to significant results over time. Imagine arriving at work, faced with a mountain of tasks. Starting with a manageable, attainable goal can set a positive tempo for the rest of the day, creating an upward spiral of productivity and well-being.

Small wins are the modest progress points that we often overlook, yet they are powerful catalysts for positive change. When we methodically carve out tasks and tick them off one by one, we create a virtuous cycle where each little success fuels the confidence and motivation needed for the next challenge. This method does not require grand gestures or herculean efforts; it thrives on simple, tangible achievements that become the building blocks of larger ambitions.

Begin by identifying a goal that is integral to your work but isn't daunting in scope. It might be clearing your inbox, completing a report, or simply organizing your workspace. By construing your tasks into manageable pieces, you shift your psychological response to work from one of overwhelm to one of achievement. A completed task, no matter how small, symbolizes progress and asserts control over your environment.

To best utilize the strategy of small wins, it needs to become habitual. Incorporating them into your daily routine ensures a consistent pattern of accomplishments that can steadily increase in complexity and significance. Making a habit of achieving small wins requires that you set specific, measurable, achievable, relevant, and time-bound (S-M-A-R-T) objectives. This methodology enables you to pinpoint the smaller steps necessary to fulfill your broader work goals.

Fostering an awareness of your accomplishments is vital for momentum. Each time a small win is achieved, take a moment to acknowledge it. This might mean pausing briefly to appreciate the completion of a task or jotting down the win in a journal. The act of recognition serves as a psychological reward that reinforces your desire to continue along this fruitful path.

Visualization is also an invaluable tool in the pursuit of small wins. When you imagine the successful completion of a task, you mentally rehearse the steps needed to achieve it. This rehearsal serves not just as motivation but also as a planning resource, providing clarity on the best course of action to reach your mini-milestones.

Balancing urgency and importance is key to ensuring that small wins are meaningful. Concentrate not only on tasks that can be swiftly accomplished but also on those that significantly impact your overall objectives. This balance ensures that each small win isn't just another checked box, but a step towards something greater.

Collaboration can often enhance the impact of small wins. Share your goals with a colleague or supervisor and seek their input. This accountability can heighten your commitment. Additionally, co-creating small wins with team members can magnify the sense of accomplishment and foster a collaborative spirit in the workplace.

Remember, achieving small wins is not about perfection. It's about progress. Mistakes and setbacks are part and parcel of the process, serving as feedback rather than failure. When a particular small win seems elusive, reframe the challenge, adapt your strategy, and press forward. Resilience in the face of obstacles is itself a small win worth celebrating.

Technology can play a supportive role in tracking and achieving small wins. Use task management apps to record and organize your daily goals. Checking off completed items digitally can provide a visual acknowledgment of your progress, much like a to-do list but with the added benefit of technology's reminders and organizational capabilities.

At the end of each day, reflect on the small wins you've accumulated. Consider how they contribute to the broader canvas of your career and personal growth. Reflection not only offers a sense of satisfaction but also helps you pivot and adjust your strategies as needed for future tasks.

In the wider picture, small wins help mitigate feelings of stress and anxiety. By breaking the day into conquerable segments, you reduce the psychological burden of an overarching, seemingly insurmountable workload. Each victory, however modest, diminishes the shadows cast by stress, illuminating a path forward with each step.

Over time, the compounding effect of regularly achieving small wins can lead to significant advancements in your career. They become the micro-habits that sculpt your professional identity, enhance your capabilities, and contribute to a fulfilling work-life balance. An accumulation of these wins demonstrates your proficiency and reliability to your peers and supervisors, potentially opening doors to more significant opportunities and recognition.

As you master the art of crafting and accomplishing small wins, share the strategy with others. Encourage colleagues to recognize and celebrate their own small wins, thereby cultivating an environment where everyone's daily victories contribute to a positive, productive workplace culture.

Embrace the power of small wins as part of your workday mantra. They are the stepping stones to career satisfaction, personal well-being, and the thriving professional life you aspire to lead. Each small victory is a brushstroke on the canvas of your life, so choose them wisely and paint your masterpiece one stroke at a time.

The Role of Rewards in Sustaining Effort

There's something irresistible about the promise of a reward—it beckons to us with the tantalizing allure of recognition and fulfillment. In the context of work, the right rewards can bridge the gap between effort and satisfaction, propelling us forward in our pursuit of happiness, productivity, and balance. We often measure the value of our labor not only by what we accomplish but also by what we receive in return. It is within this dynamic exchange that rewards assume their pivotal role in sustaining our efforts.

Rewards serve as a beacon, a guiding light that adds clarity to the goal ahead. When you're tasked with navigating through the tumultuous seas of strenuous workloads and tight deadlines, the reward is the lighthouse signaling safe harbor. This sustenance of effort through the anticipation of rewards can transform the mundane into the extraordinary; it can make the arduous journey not just bearable, but desirable.

Many might wonder, 'What exactly constitutes a reward?' The answer is deeply personal and varies remarkably from individual to individual. For some, the notion of a reward is intrinsically tied to monetary compensation—an unequivocal acknowledgment of one's value in currency. For others, a true reward might be recognition, whether through a compliment from a respected peer or a public accolade that underlines one's competence and contribution.

To foster a rewarding atmosphere, embracing a variety of reward types is key. It allows for personal preferences and ensures that different motivations are catered to. After all, diversity in rewards bolsters the recognition that we don't all sail the same emotional or psychological seas; we're enlivened by different winds and steered by different stars.

Another facet of the reward system is immediacy. The swifter the reward follows the effort, the more potent its impact. Delay can dull the luster of a reward, making it seem less connected to the work one has invested. There's an undeniable satisfaction in completing a task and promptly reaping the attendant benefits, an action-reward cycle that resonates deeply within us.

Yet, it's not just about the size or the speed of the bounty; it's the frequency too. Small, consistent rewards can create a cadence, a rhythm to our work lives that sustains momentum. Not every task can or will end with grand fanfare, but the subtle symphony of mini-rewards can compound into an epic score, spurring continued engagement with our labors.

However, there exists a delicate balance in the world of rewards: over-reliance on external rewards can diminish intrinsic motivation. It's crucial to foster an environment where the work itself becomes rewarding, where the process and mastery of skills are just as celebrated as the outcome. The most durable dedication comes from finding joy and purpose in the work we do, creating a self-sustaining cycle of effort and satisfaction.

Recognizing our own needs for rewards is an exercise in self-awareness. It requires an examination of our desires and what truly drives us. Are we seeking validation, growth, comfort, or perhaps a blend of many elements? By understanding our personal reward mechanisms, we can set up systems and pursue avenues at work that resonate with our internal compass—a compass that guides us through challenges with resilience.

Reflecting on the rewards that have meant the most to us can be enlightening. Was it the monetary bonus, the extra day off, or the hand-written note from a team leader that made us feel most appreciated? Identifying these memorable rewards can inform future strategies for sustaining effort and ensuring that the rewards we seek—and those we offer to others—are meaningful and effective.

Let's also consider the timing of rewards. Just as a well-timed meal can satiate our hunger before it becomes unbearable, a well-timed reward can rejuvenate our spirits before they dwindle. Employers and leaders can look to implement reward systems that acknowledge the natural ebbs and flows of work energy, pitching in a boost exactly when it's most needed.

The beauty of rewards lies in their transformative power. They can turn the solitary toil of a difficult project into a shared victory, binding a team together. Collaborative efforts often culminate in collective rewards, which not only serve to celebrate a job well done but also foster a sense of unity and shared purpose.

As we strive to sustain effort both within ourselves and amongst our colleagues, it's essential to appreciate the impact that rewards can have on our well-being. They're more than just prizes or bonuses at the end of a tunnel of toil; they're acknowledgments of our humanity, our need to feel seen, and our desire to know that what we do matters. It is this recognition that often carries us through to the next peak.

An overlooked aspect of rewards is their communicative power. They send a message about what is valued within a team or organization. Rewards that align with core values and mission statements reinforce company culture and ideals, solidifying a sense of identity and purpose. They tell a story of what is celebrated and what is encouraged to flourish within the workplace community.

While crafting reward systems, it is necessary to maintain fairness and transparency. Perceptions of favoritism or inconsistent reward distribution can fracture the very foundation on which the mechanism aims to build. An objective and clear reward structure ensures that everyone knows what is expected and what is at stake, fostering a workplace that is harmonious and just.

The role of rewards in sustaining effort is multifaceted and profound. Rewards give us a taste of the future and offer solace for the struggles of the present. When designed thoughtfully, rewards can uplift spirits, enhance performance and cultivate a well-balanced work life that aligns with our deepest motivations. As we climb various ladders of achievement, it is the rewards along the way that can sustain our climb and make the view from the top all the more rewarding.

Finding Your Why: Connecting Work to Personal Goals

Within the labyrinth of our daily routines, it's vital we carve out a path that leads not just to the completion of immediate tasks, but also to the realization of our deeply held personal goals. The question of why we do what we do—our purpose at work—is the silent engine powering our motivation, shaping our vision, and fostering our resilience. In this pursuit, identifying your 'why' transforms your professional journey into an extension of your personal narrative, inviting a sense of fulfillment that transcends the mere tally of hours and achievements.

The connection between work and personal aspirations can seem weak at first glance—after all, isn't work often just a means to an end? Yet in reality, the tightrope between professional duties and personal satisfaction is walked by weaving together the strands of what matters most to us. When your daily work reflects your values, helps you grow towards your dreams, or allows you to contribute in a way that is meaningful, your job becomes more than just a paycheck; it becomes a chapter in your larger life story.

To discover your 'why', begin by reflecting on your life's peaks and valleys. Consider the moments when you have felt most alive, engaged, or proud. What were you doing? Who were you helping? What impact did you have? These reflections are your compass, pointing towards the values and passions that can guide your professional endeavors.

Once you've gleaned insights into what drives you, it's time to examine your current role. Does your work allow you to leverage your strengths and honor your values? Perhaps you find meaning through innovation, solving complex problems, or helping others. By laying bare the aspects of your job that resonate with these driving forces, you can begin to tailor your responsibilities—and even your career trajectory—to better align with your personal goals.

Importantly, connecting work to personal aspirations is not a one-size-fits-all task. It requires introspection and honesty. Are your goals for material gain, personal development, creative expression, or social impact? Defining clear, personal objectives makes it easier to see how your nine-to-five efforts contribute to these broader aims.

Another crucial step is setting goals that are both aspirational and achievable. This dual focus acts as an anchor, keeping you grounded when the waters of workplace chaos swell but also hoisting your sails to catch the wind of opportunity. Progress towards these goals should be measurable, so you can visually chart your advancement and find joy in the journey.

Sometimes the bridge between personal aims and professional duties needs a touch of creativity. You might not find direct channels through which your work feeds your goals. In such cases, look for indirect links. For instance, your job could be developing a skill that is a stepping stone toward your broader aspirations, or perhaps it's providing the resources that allow you to pursue your passions outside of office hours.

When alignment between work and personal ambitions feels out of reach, communication with supervisors or mentors can pave the way. A culture of open dialogue allows you to express your desire for tasks or projects that are more in sync with your personal goals. It's possible that opportunities for alignment exist, but your leaders are simply unaware of your aspirations.

Also, learning how to effectively advocate for yourself within your work environment is essential. It could mean negotiating for roles that suit your strengths, suggesting new initiatives that you're passionate about, or even creating your position within the company that marries your talents with organizational needs.

Find comfort in knowing that your 'why' is not static; it evolves as you grow personally and professionally. The dynamic nature of your 'why' means that your job need not be a perfect fit at every moment. What's crucial is staying mindful of your evolving goals and being ready to pivot or make changes as necessary.

It's also worth considering that happiness at work is not solely contingent on job roles but also on the relationships and community cultivated within the workplace. A sense of belonging and contribution to a team can amplify personal fulfillment, reflecting our inherent social nature and desire for connection.

In time, the synergy between your career and personal ambitions can turn your professional life into a source of profound happiness. Beyond elevating your mood, it enhances your productivity and can dramatically reduce stress levels. After all, when we see how each task contributes to our life's larger tapestry, we approach our work with greater enthusiasm and persistence.

However, be prepared for challenges and be willing to reassess periodically. Just as a sailor adjusts sails to changes in the wind, you must be willing to realign work with your evolving 'why'. This could entail further education, a change in occupation, or even a leap of faith into entrepreneurship.

Ultimately, by finding and connecting with your 'why', you're not just forging a pathway to success—you're crafting a life brimming with passion, purpose, and personal fulfillment. Work becomes not a mere act of survival, but an enriching endeavor that feeds your soul and propels you towards your most cherished dreams.

It's evident that when work aligns with personal goals, the benefits are multifaceted. Not only does it breed a deeper engagement and satisfaction in your career, but it also establishes the foundation for a more balanced, joyful, and stress-managed life. This alignment is a continuous and deliberate effort—a journey well worth embarking on for anyone who seeks to blend their work with their essence.

Chapter 6:
Stress Reduction Techniques

In the hustle of a workday, it's easy to find ourselves tangled in stress webs that seem to tighten with every passing minute. Aware as we are of its grip, we often struggle to discover effective strategies to break free. However, with intention and practice, reducing workplace stress can become a manageable, if not enriching, endeavor. Understanding the salient tactics for alleviating this tension can transform our professional lives.

Begin with the timeless wisdom of harnessing the power of exercise for stress relief. Physical activity stimulates the release of endorphins, those biochemical messengers of comfort, which play an essential role in the elevation of mood and reduction of pain. Whether it's a brisk walk during lunch, a before-work jog, or a yoga session infused throughout your day, incorporating movement into your routine is pivotal for stress management.

However, invigorating the body doesn't have to be an exhaustive marathon. Consistently injecting small doses of activity can yield significant dividends. Simple approaches such as standing stretches or desk-based exercises can punctuate your day with vitality and fend off the physical manifestations of stress.

Equally essential is embracing the importance of regular breaks. Rapid-fire tasks and ceaseless emails can tax the most resilient of minds. The strategic pausing of labor, not just physically but mentally, allows for restoration. Short, frequent breaks have been shown to boost creativity and productivity while safeguarding mental health.

Consider these intermissions sacred; step away from the digital world and immerse in moments of quiet reverence. Perhaps you might find solace in a cup of tea enjoyed away from the screen's glow, or the meditative rhythm of a walk where you allow thoughts to flow freely without the need to capture or act upon them.

Amid trying times, we mustn't undervalue the sanctuary of relationships. Seeking support from peers and mentors introduces external perspectives that can alleviate the blind spots stress often creates. These allies in our journey can offer encouragement, actionable advice, or even just the empathetic ear needed to verbalize and process the pressures at hand.

Shared experiences foster a sense of belonging and collective resilience. There's exceptional potency in being part of a community where stressors are recognized and confronted as a collective rather than individuals in isolation. Regular check-ins with colleagues and mentors serve as a conduit for support and empathy.

Stress can be a cunning adversary, often disguising itself until it has woven itself tightly into our daily tapestry. Hence, proactive engagement in stress reduction is paramount. This might involve creating rituals that signal the start and end of your workday, thus establishing psychological boundaries that help contain work-induced stress.

Routines have the dual power of providing structure and serving as comforting constants amidst the chaos. They can be as transformative as bookending your day with meditation, journaling, or simply tidying your workspace to maintain a sense of control and order.

Flexibility, too, is a crucial ally. Rigidity in self-imposed rules can sometimes add to our burden. Being gentle with ourselves, allowing for modifications in our routines as needed, can foster resilience while preventing additional strain.

In the quest for tranquility, the power of visualization often goes understated. Envisioning oneself navigating a stressful situation with poise and confidence can set a blueprint for the actual experience. Imagining a protective bubble around oneself that repels stress can offer a much-needed reminder of personal strength and autonomy.

Moreover, the pursuit of stress mastery is incomplete without nurturing nourishing self-dialogue. The narratives we tell ourselves can either deflate our spirit or become wind beneath our wings. Crafting an internal discourse that is forgiving, encouraging, and hopeful primes us for a healthier engagement with our professional challenges.

Yet stress reduction is not an isolated endeavor. It extends beyond the individual to the environment. Thus, customizing our workspace to serve as a refuge from the racket of office hustle can mark an important stride in mitigating stress. Elements as simple as plants, personal pictures, or even a preferred layout can provide comfort and a semblance of personal space.

In a greater context, it's vital to appreciate the subtleties of consistent practice. Stress reduction is not a one-time event but a skill honed through regular application. It's the consistent thread through the fabric of our professional lives, one that requires attention and dedication to maintain and strengthen.

Ultimately, the journey to less stress in the workplace is as much about the techniques we employ as it is about our commitment to them. It requires both the acknowledgment of stress's presence and the continuous effort to engage practices that weave calm into our work tapestry. Each step, each breath, each break is a stitch in a grander motif of well-being and professional fulfillment.

With this chapter laying the groundwork, let us proceed with the understanding that managing stress is not a passive resignation to external forces but an active dance of adjustment, balance, and a celebration of the quiet triumphs in the dynamic arena of work life.

Exercise as Stress Relief As the workday folds into an eve, many feel the toll it has taken, not just on their minds but on their bodies as well. The stress from looming deadlines, the constant ping of notifications, and interoffice dynamics can seep into our muscles and our marrow. It begs for release and that's where exercise comes not merely as a remedy but as a powerful alchemist, transmuting the leaden weight of the day's worries into the gold of vitality and calm.

Let's start with the basics; movement is essential to human health. Our ancestors spent their days walking, hunting, and gathering—constant motion was a necessity of life. Today's sedentary style sharply contrasts with their active lifestyle. Despite this evolution, our bodies still long for movement. Exercise releases a cascade of natural chemicals in our brain, such as endorphins and serotonin, that elevate our mood and dissipate tension. This is not just conjecture—it's a fact as solid and grounded as the earth beneath our running shoes.

When we speak of exercise, it's not a one-size-fits-all prescription. The beauty lies in diversity—running, yoga, weightlifting, dancing—the options are as limitless as imagination itself. This is empowerment, the freedom to choose the form of physical activity that resonates with your soul. Not everyone will find serenity in the whir of a bicycle wheel; some might find it in the rhythmic counting of a weight set. The key is consistent engagement in whichever form speaks to you personally.

Consistency, however, can be elusive in a world where time is like a cup overfilling with demands. Setting aside time for exercise can seem daunting, but integrating movement into your day doesn't require monumental shifts. A simple walk during lunch, taking the stairs instead of the elevator, or a short bodyweight circuit in the morning can make a dramatic impact. Small ripples create big waves. It's the daily commitment that can morph into a formidable force against stress.

The mental clarity that emerges post-exercise is not a mythic state—it's acutely tangible. As the heart pumps more swiftly, sending oxygen coursing through veins to the brain, there's a sharpening of focus, a clarifying of thought. This biological response doesn't merely provide a fleeting reprieve but can fuel a more sustained period of productivity and calm.

Moreover, scheduled exercise can be an anchor point in your day. Planning for a workout instills a sense of routine and predictability that can counterbalance the unpredictable nature of work challenges. Here lies a paradox: within the fixed ritual of exercise, you find flexibility—mental suppleness to deal with the unexpected, the capacity to pivot with poise when work throws a curveball.

It's also worth celebrating the social aspect of exercise. Group classes or team sports can foster community and camaraderie, offering a counterweight to isolation that stressful workplaces can sometimes engender. Within these groups, support systems are born. They become shields not just against the physical demands of activity but against the strains of the day-to-day grind.

When the mind wrestles with stress, sleep often bears the brunt of the struggle. Regular physical exertion fosters a deep, restorative sleep. The gentle sway of the resting body after a day augmented by exercise is akin to the calm that blankets a forest after a gusty storm. The quality of sleep post-exercise can aid in resetting the stress response, so the new day's challenges are met with renewed vigor and resilience.

The empowerment drawn from mastering a physical skill or reaching a fitness goal can spill over into work life as well. Each personal record, each extra mile, each held yoga pose, redefines the boundaries of personal capability.

These triumphs whisper to the subconscious that perhaps, the limitations at work are as surmountable as those in the gym or on the track.

It's this very transference of confidence that makes exercise so potent as a stress-relief tool. The correlation isn't just about the physiological. It is about reimagining the very narrative of one's life. You're not just a worker, a title, a role—you are a being capable of growth, change, and achievement, both in and outside the confines of the office.

Engaging in nature too can amplify the effects of exercise. The very act of inhaling fresh air, of being surrounded by the tapestry of the outdoors, can act as a salve to work-induced stress. Just as a tree bends and sways with the wind yet remains rooted, so can outdoor activities remind us to remain grounded, yet adaptable.

Additionally, exercise can act as a mediator for mindfulness. It provides the space to observe thoughts without attachment, to let the carousel of worries slow to a standstill. Whether it's the repetition of laps in a pool or the order of a strength training routine, there is a meditative quality inherent in these patterns. This meditation in motion is conducive to a state where stress exists, but doesn't overwhelm.

Let's not also forget that when we consider the wellness of our physical form, it affects how we present ourselves to the world. A posture bred from physical strength carries an unmistakable message of confidence. When stress endeavors to make one small, to shrink one's being, the stature afforded by regular exercise is a visual and visceral defiance.

In the convergence of the physiological and the psychological benefits of exercise lie the seeds of a more holistic approach to work stress. Exercise isn't just a reaction to stress; it's a proactive measure. It is a declaration of the importance of self-care, an affirmation that you have agency over your well-being amidst the demands of productivity.

Exercise as stress relief is not a cure-all. It won't dissolve all woes or untangle every knot of tension that work can weave. Yet, in the same breath, to ignore its potency is to deny oneself a formidable ally in the quest for balance between the demands of work and the necessity for personal peace. It is a tool, sharpened by will and wielded with intent, that can carve out a sanctuary of serenity in the most turbulent of professional storms.

The Importance of Regular Breaks In the intricate dance of productivity and well-being, the rhythm is often set by the most underappreciated element: the humble break. Just as the heart sustains life with its ceaseless beat and periodic rest, so too must the dedicated worker recognize the inherent value of stepping away from the never-ending to-do list.

Consider the beat of your workday not as relentless, but as a series of sprints and rests. This structure isn't merely about survival; it's about thriving. Regular breaks are not just pauses; they are part and parcel of the work itself. They restore our mental clarity and revitalize our motivation, turning what could be a grueling marathon into a series of manageable intervals.

It's a biological imperative to take breaks. Our cognitive machinery is designed for bursts of focused activity followed by rest. Studies have shown that without regular downtime, our ability to concentrate, remember, and be creative suffers greatly. A break is a time when the mind can meander, free from the constraints of concentrated thinking, allowing for a subconscious processing that often leads to eureka moments.

Moreover, regular breaks help in maintaining a healthier physical state. Sitting for long hours is dubbed the new smoking for good reason. It can lead to an array of health issues, from cardiovascular problems to muscle degradation. Short, regular breaks that include physical movement can mitigate these risks, keeping the body's circulation flowing and muscles engaged.

But how does one disengage without feeling the tug of guilt or the fear of falling behind? The answer lies in mindful planning. Intentional breaks, scheduled as a crucial segment of the day, are a commitment to oneself. They are the acknowledgement that to work smart is to work sustainably, and to work sustainably is to embrace the rhythm of effort and ease.

Mental health, often swept under the rug in the professional realm, benefits significantly from these pauses. Mental fatigue can lead to burnout – a state of emotional, physical, and mental exhaustion caused by excessive and prolonged stress. By allowing time to decompress throughout the day, we maintain not only our performance but also our emotional equilibrium.

Yet there's a societal myth that must be dispelled: the illusion that constant work equals productivity. This not only harms our efficiency but also our sense of joy and accomplishment. When you allow yourself regular respites, you give space for appreciation, reflection, and reassessment of the tasks at hand.

Another facet of breaks that is often overlooked is their impact on creativity. When we step back, we allow for a broader view of our work. We can connect dots that seemed unrelated and approach problems with newfound perspective. Regular breaks thus act as incubators for innovation and creativity.

Interpersonal relationships at work, too, get a boost from shared break times. Casual conversations in the break room can lead to stronger connections and can foster a sense of community and support that is invaluable in any workplace.

So what do these breaks look like in practice? They don't have to be lengthy or elaborate. A stroll around the office, a moment of quiet meditation, or simply stepping outside for a breath of fresh air can be rejuvenating. The key is to unplug from the task at hand, allowing your senses to reset and recharge.

This brings into focus an essential reality: the need for discipline. Taking regular breaks requires self-discipline not to be lured into the vortex of constant connectivity and digital distraction. It is a conscious effort to claim time for restorative practices that serve your productivity in the long run.

Breaks are not a sign of weakness or inefficiency. Quite the opposite – they can be strategic tools that propel you towards greater accomplishments. By pacing yourself with thoughtfully timed pauses, you can harness the full potential of your skills and labor with a clear mind and a recharged spirit.

The pattern and timing of breaks are as individual as the person taking them. There's a cadence to cultivating the right balance between toil and rest. Some may thrive on the classic technique of the Pomodoro method, working for 25 minutes and then taking a 5-minute break. Others may find a 90-minute work session followed by a 15-minute break aligns better with their natural rhythms.

And let's not forget the significance of longer breaks - lunch hours, days off, and vacations. They serve as milestones that punctuate our work life, offering extended periods to relax, reflect, and reinvigorate our sense of purpose and passion for the work we do.

Ultimately, embracing the importance of regular breaks is about respecting the intricate mechanisms of mind and body. This respectful acknowledgment of our human limitations and potentials can lead to a transformation in the way we work – a transformation towards a healthier, happier, and more productive life within and beyond the office walls. Let the rhythm of breaks in your workday be a source of strength, not a stumbling block, and watch as your capacity for sustained productivity blossoms in kind.

Seeking Support from Peers and Mentors

As we navigate the complex terrain of work, we inevitably encounter stressors that strain our resilience. To bolster our well-being and achieve balance, the wisdom and empathy of peers and mentors can serve as an anchor amidst the storm. Recognizing the value in shared experiences, it is essential to cultivate relationships that foster mutual support and growth within a professional setting.

Peers at work provide more than just camaraderie; they are witnesses to the daily challenges we face. By engaging with colleagues, one can find solace in understanding that these obstacles are not borne alone. Establishing a trusted network of peers opens the door for meaningful exchanges of strategies to tackle stress and workload management.

It's not just about venting frustrations, but creating a space for constructive conversation and feedback. Within such circles, vulnerabilities can be shared without fear of judgment, thus promoting a sense of communal resilience.

Mentorship, on the other hand, brings the invaluable insights of those who have tread similar paths before us. The guidance of a mentor can help us navigate career development, manage personal ambitions, and maintain a healthy perspective on professional challenges. A mentor's experiences equip them to offer tailored advice and encouragement that can illuminate the path ahead.

Seeking mentorship can be a formal arrangement within an organization or an informal relationship nurtured over time. The key is to approach mentors with clear intentions and a willingness to learn and apply their advice. The relationship should be built on respect, commitment, and shared values, creating a safe environment for growth and learning.

Engaging with mentors also offers a unique opportunity to improve emotional intelligence—

understanding how to process and manage emotions in professional contexts. As mentors often share their own stories, we can benefit from their coping strategies for maintaining emotional equilibrium during high-pressure situations.

In the process of seeking support, don't overlook the power of peer mentorship. This can be especially effective in tight-knit teams where members rotate leadership and support roles. Peer mentors may more closely relate to one's immediate work experience and offer more readily applicable advice.

Creating a mentorship or support network need not be a daunting task. Simple measures like joining professional social groups, participating in industry-related discussions, or reaching out to someone whose career trajectory you admire, can all be starting points. Even within your immediate work environment, engaging more deeply with colleagues can spark mentoring relationships.

Keep in mind that mentorship is a two-way street. As much as you gain from a mentor's knowledge, sharing your own experiences contributes to their understanding of changing trends and fresh perspectives. This reciprocal exchange enriches the mentor-mentee dynamic and strengthens professional networks.

Additionally, workshops and training sessions often present natural opportunities to develop supportive relationships. Attending these events with the intention to connect can lay the groundwork for significant peer and mentor support structures.

Online platforms have also expanded the reach of supportive professional networks. Digital mentorship and peer support communities abound, granting access to a diverse array of expertise and experiences beyond geographic limitations.

However, it's crucial to maintain boundaries and professional etiquette when participating in these communities. A respectful discourse and sensitivity to confidentiality ensure that all parties feel secure and valued in the exchange.

Remember that the goal of seeking support is not just to survive the workday but to thrive within it. Incorporating perspectives beyond one's own broadens the toolkit for problem-solving, fosters innovation, and nurtures a sense of belonging in the workplace.

As you build these relationships, consider how your role within your network might evolve over time. Today's mentee may be tomorrow's mentor, and learning to offer support to others is just as vital as seeking it. By acknowledging the reciprocal nature of these relationships, we solidify the foundation for a collaborative and supportive work environment.

Nurturing these relationships during calm periods is just as crucial as leaning on them during times of stress. Investing time and energy into maintaining your network ensures that it will be there when you need it most, and serves as a testament to the collective strength shared among professionals striving for a harmonious work-life balance.

The journey towards happiness and satisfaction at work is one best traveled with companions who understand the landscape. Peers and mentors not only provide a supportive sounding board but also help to construct a roadmap filled with insights, cautionary tales, and encouragement to persevere. By seeking out and valuing these relationships, we fortify our ability to remain steadfast and agile in the ever-evolving world of work.

Chapter 7: Navigating Interpersonal Challenges at Work

The terrain of our professional lives isn't just strewn with the obvious hurdles of deadlines and projects; it's often the interpersonal dynamics that are the most challenging to navigate. The way we interact with our colleagues, manage relationships with superiors, and defuse conflicts contributes significantly to our workplace happiness and productivity. Interpersonal challenges require a nuanced approach, as every individual in your work sphere brings their unique mix of experiences and emotions to the table.

Those difficult coworkers we encounter can certainly set the stage for stress, yet we must consider that their behavior often stems from their own battles and insecurities. Approach these situations with empathy while maintaining clear boundaries. To effectively deal with challenging colleagues, focus on the behavior affecting your work, address issues directly and professionally, and seek to find common ground.

Remember, the goal isn't to change them, but rather to find a way to collaborate effectively despite the differences.

Perhaps even more daunting is the task of managing up, particularly when faced with a supervisor whose leadership style edges into toxicity. The power dynamics at play can make this a treacherous path. In such instances, it's critical to proactively protect your well-being. Document interactions, seek the support of HR if necessary, and develop a coping strategy; perhaps establishing a mentoring relationship outside your immediate reporting line could provide a buffer and guidance.

When conflicts arise it's essential to arm yourself with resolution skills. Take a thoughtful stance in resolving disagreements, focusing on discussing behaviors and outcomes rather than personalities. Listen actively, and express your perspective without assigning blame. Remember that conflict, when managed appropriately, can lead to growth, innovation, and greater understanding between workers.

It's not uncommon to feel like navigating these interpersonal challenges is an insurmountable task, but it's these very experiences that can fortify you with resilience and adaptability. Align yourself with a strong sense of purpose at work, using your personal goals as a compass to guide you through difficult interactions. This perspective helps in maintaining a sense of control and fulfillment regardless of the complex human dynamics that come into play.

Communication is undoubtedly the cornerstone of healthy relationships in the workplace. Developing clear communication skills can prevent a multitude of misunderstandings and conflicts. Ensure that you are being heard and understood, all while affording your colleagues the same courtesy. This back-and-forth, when done with respect and clarity, can turn even the most challenging interactions into opportunities for professional development and problem-solving.

Mentorship is another invaluable tool in dealing with social issues at work. Seek guidance from mentors who have been in your shoes and can offer you the wisdom of their experiences. Not only can they provide practical advice for handling complex relationships, but they can also be a comforting reminder that you're not alone in facing these challenges.

In critical moments, remember to take a step back and approach the situation from a place of mindfulness. This allows you to respond rather than react—a subtle but powerful distinction that can diffuse potential conflicts. By cultivating a mindfulness practice, you develop the emotional intelligence necessary to manage interpersonal challenges with grace.

Moreover, never underestimate the power of self-care and its role in maintaining composure in the face of interpersonal stressors. Make self-care a non-negotiable part of your routine; it provides the mental and emotional space necessary to handle work relationships with patience and insight.

In essence, navigating the interpersonal challenges at work isn't just about dealing with others—it's also about managing ourselves. As you work through this chapter, you will gain tools and strategies not just to survive these challenges but to thrive amid them. This continuous journey of learning how to relate effectively with those around you at work is a critical part of your quest for happiness, productivity, stress management, and work-life balance.

Dealing with Difficult Coworkers Gritting your teeth and tightening your grip on a coffee cup that's gone cold—this might be a familiar scene when dealing with challenging colleagues. At some point in our careers, we encounter individuals whose behaviors, work styles, or communication patterns clash with our own. These interactions can lead to increased stress and decreased happiness in our work environment. But rather than allowing difficult coworkers to cast a shadow on our professional life, let's explore strategies to stand our ground with grace and maintain our productivity and well-being.

In the landscape of workplace relationships, understanding is our compass. Before labeling a coworker as difficult, we need to step back and attempt to see the world from their perspective. Perhaps they are dealing with personal stressors or are unaware of the impact of their actions. By acknowledging that there might be unseen factors at play, we cultivate a mindset that seeks to understand rather than judge, opening a pathway to empathy and, ultimately, more effective communication.

Effective communication is, unsurprisingly, a cornerstone of managing difficult relationships. Engaging in open, honest, yet respectful dialogue can sometimes dissipate tension and clarify misunderstandings. When initiating this conversation, aim to express feelings without placing blame using 'I' statements—these will reduce the likelihood of defensive reactions and keep the focus on resolving the issue at hand.

Boundaries play a critical role in protecting our well-being amidst workplace challenges. It's essential to establish and maintain boundaries clearly and consistently with all coworkers, not just the difficult ones. This might mean declining last-minute requests that interfere with your personal time or saying 'no' to additional tasks when your plate is already full. Strong boundaries allow us to assert our needs while still being a cooperative team member.

If direct communication and boundary setting haven't smoothed the waters, it's time to strategize. Try to minimize your contact with the difficult coworker if possible. Whether it means requesting a seat change, adjusting your work schedule, or finding alternative ways to complete tasks, reducing interactions can decrease the occurrence of stress-inducing episodes.

When interactions are unavoidable, prepare yourself mentally. Before heading into a meeting or project with this person, spend a few moments grounding yourself with deep breathing or envisioning a positive outcome. By centering yourself, you can approach the situation with calm and prevent emotional responses from taking the wheel.

Stress management techniques, such as those discussed in earlier chapters on exercise and mindfulness, can be invaluable tools in coping with difficult coworkers. Consistently incorporating these practices into your daily routine will not only reduce the stress associated with challenging individuals but can enhance your resilience and emotional intelligence, equipping you better to handle interpersonal conflicts.

Sometimes, despite our best efforts, we might still find ourselves overwhelmed. In these situations, it's wise to lean on a support system. Discussing your challenges with a trusted peer or mentor can provide fresh perspectives and validation. They might offer coping strategies you hadn't considered or provide the encouragement needed to persevere in the relationship.

Don't forget to document your encounters if they escalate to harassment or bullying. Keeping a record of dates, times, and descriptions of interactions provides clear evidence should you need to involve human resources or your supervisor. Remember, there's a difference between everyday workplace challenges and toxic, abusive behavior. Recognize the line and be prepared to escalate when necessary.

Another key strategy is to focus on collaboration. By nurturing a culture of cooperation in the workplace, we often find that many issues with difficult coworkers can be alleviated. Actively seeking to include those individuals in team projects and discussions can foster a sense of belonging and potentially reduce friction by showing them they're valued members of the group.

It's also crucial to practice detachment. By depersonalizing the situation and understanding that their behavior is not a reflection of you, you can maintain a level of emotional distance that preserves your inner peace. This detachment allows you to interact with the coworker without becoming entangled in the negativity their behavior might inspire.

In the quest to maintain happiness at work, remember that we can't change others, but we can adjust our responses. Focusing on what you can control, such as your attitude and actions, can substantially mitigate the effects of a difficult coworker on your overall well-being and satisfaction.

If all else fails, and the situation becomes unreasonable, consider discussing the matter with your supervisor or human resources. When doing so, stick to the facts and maintain professionalism. It's important that your concerns are taken seriously and not seen as mere complaints.

Take time to reflect and consider whether you can learn something from the situation. Interpersonal challenges often come with valuable lessons about communication, resilience, and self-awareness. By reflecting on what you can learn, you can turn even the most challenging coworker relationship into an opportunity for personal growth.

As we navigate the choppy waters of workplace relationships, maintaining a commitment to our own well-being, implementing sound communication strategies, and staying true to our values can help us emerge more capable and centered professionals. Let's acknowledge the complexity of human interactions, but not allow it to diminish our happiness at work. Instead, let's embrace the challenge as part of our journey to become better communicators, more compassionate colleagues, and resilient individuals thriving in our careers.

Managing Up: Handling Toxic Supervisors

Engaging with a supervisor who emanates toxicity can feel like maneuvering through a field laden with hidden pitfalls. The challenge is formidable, yet surmountable with a blend of strategic composure and interpersonal savvy. This section delves into the nuanced art of managing up when faced with the difficult situation of a toxic supervisor.

It's imperative to recognize and accept that you can't change a person's inherent nature, especially in a supervisory role. However, you do have control over how you respond to their behavior. The ability to maintain a cool head and respond rather than react can be a considerable asset. Reflect on the idea that your calmness isn't just for your benefit, but it can also serve as a mitigating influence on your supervisor's behavior.

Building a buffer of emotional detachment is essential. When every criticism or snide remark feels like a personal slight, it can be easy to spiral into negativity. Instead, try to view interactions with a level of professional detachment, separating your self-worth from your supervisor's behavior. Focus on the objective quality of your work and the value you bring to the team.

Diligently documenting interactions can serve as both a defensive strategy and a means to gain clarity on the patterns of behavior you're dealing with. Notes on dates, times, and specifics of exchanges provide a solid foundation should you need to escalate the issue to human resources. Moreover, keeping a record can sometimes reveal insights into triggers and potential strategies for avoiding the most toxic displays.

Prioritize open and assertive communication, even when it feels counterintuitive. Many toxic supervisors thrive on ambiguity and unstated expectations. By clearly discussing work tasks, deadlines, and feedback methods, you can reduce the chances of misunderstandings that might prompt toxic behavior.

It's also vital to set and enforce your own boundaries. Identify what you're willing to tolerate and what actions will prompt you to seek support or report the behavior. Knowing when to say no, or when to call out inappropriate conduct, is crucial in preserving your well-being.

Seek allies within the workplace. Building relationships with other colleagues or mentors can provide a support network when dealing with a toxic supervisor. These allies can offer advice, provide emotional support, and potentially advocate on your behalf.

Focusing on your professional growth can sometimes provide solace from the stress of a toxic supervisor. Instead of ruminating on negative interactions, channel your energy into learning new skills or volunteering for projects that can enhance your resume. This not only benefits your career trajectory but can also boost your morale.

Exploring other opportunities can also be empowering. If the situation seems intractable, looking for a new position either within the company or externally can provide hope and an eventual exit from the toxicity. This doesn't mean you should jump ship at the first sign of trouble, but recognizing when it's time to move on can be a form of taking control.

Consider utilizing stress reduction techniques both inside and outside of work to manage the physical and emotional toll of working with a toxic supervisor. Whether it's exercise, mindfulness, or engaging in a fulfilling hobby, self-care is a key component in maintaining your equilibrium.

Ultimately, it's important to approach this situation with a long-term perspective. While you may not be able to immediately change your circumstances or your supervisor, developing resilience and a plan for handling toxicity can improve your current situation and prepare you for future challenges.

In some cases, formal intervention may be necessary. If all attempts to manage the situation on your own are unsuccessful and the behavior of your supervisor violates company policy or employment law, it's time to take your documentation to HR or consider discussing your situation with an employment lawyer.

Never underestimate the value of professional counseling or employee assistance programs to help navigate the emotional minefield of dealing with a toxic supervisor. External, unbiased perspectives can be invaluable in finding effective strategies to cope.

Remember to celebrate small victories along the way. Whether it means successfully navigating a difficult conversation, completing a project despite obstacles, or simply making it through a tough day, acknowledging your strength and resilience can bolster your spirits and keep you motivated.

Engaging with a toxic supervisor is undeniably taxing, but with these strategies, you can maintain your professional integrity and well-being. By staying proactive, guarding your emotional health, and preparing for the long haul, you can turn a challenging dynamic into an opportunity for profound personal growth and resilience in the workplace.

Conflict Resolution Skills In the landscape of professional relationships, conflict is an inevitable terrain. The skill to navigate these conflicts with grace and effectiveness is not just desirable but essential for maintaining happiness, productivity, and balance at work.

Our focus here is on honing those skills that will serve you in turning contentious situations into opportunities for growth and collaboration.

At the heart of conflict resolution is communication—a tool as delicate as it is powerful. Engaging in open dialogue is the cornerstone of understanding diverse perspectives. It begins with active listening, a technique that involves not just hearing words, but also interpreting the emotions and meanings behind them. Giving your full attention and acknowledging the other person's perspective can transform a potential standoff into an avenue for mutual understanding.

Once you've established a foundation of understanding, employing empathy is the next stepping stone. Empathy involves stepping into the shoes of your coworker and viewing the situation from their vantage point. This does not mean you have to agree with them but recognizing their feelings and validating their concerns can reduce defensive postures and create a space for open negotiation.

Articulating your viewpoint is just as crucial. Express your thoughts and feelings clearly and without accusation. Use "I" statements to convey your perspective without placing blame, such as "I feel overwhelmed when deadlines are changed without notice," instead of "You always mess up the schedule."

Rise Above

A collaborative approach to problem-solving is what separates mere compromise from true resolution. Rather than focusing on what each party will give up, shift your attention to how everyone can contribute to a solution that serves collective interests. This not only helps to resolve the current issue but also strengthens the relationships and trust among those involved.

Conflict can often trigger strong emotions, and it's important to manage them effectively. Techniques like taking deep breaths or requesting a pause in the conversation can help in maintaining composure. It's okay to step back if you feel too heated to continue in a productive manner. A calm, composed response is more likely to yield positive outcomes than a heated reaction.

Even with the best intentions, sometimes conflicts can edge towards escalation. Here, the skill of de-escalation becomes invaluable. Keeping your tone steady, lowering your voice, and using clear and simple language can help to dial down the intensity. Reflect on the goals of the conversation rather than individual points of contention.

Negotiation is an art. Sometimes both parties can't get everything they want, but they can get enough to be satisfied. Prioritize the issues at stake and determine where you have flexibility. Be prepared to offer alternatives that are acceptable to both parties and keep an open mind to the suggestions of others.

When progress stalls, it's beneficial to reiterate the common goal. Remind everyone that you're on the same team and that the aim is to find a solution that helps the team succeed. Refocusing on common objectives fosters a sense of shared purpose which can help reignite cooperative efforts.

After reaching a resolution, it's valuable to reflect on the conflict and learn from the experience. Assess the root causes of the dispute and consider what preventive measures can be taken in the future. Reflecting not only prevents similar situations from arising but also contributes to your personal growth and conflict management expertise.

Establishing clear agreements about the way forward cements the resolution. Document agreements when necessary and set up follow-up meetings to ensure that resolutions are implemented. This follow-through demonstrates commitment to the solution and helps to avoid misunderstandings or relapses into conflict.

Conflicts are sometimes symptomatic of larger systemic issues within the organization. If repeated conflicts arise over similar issues, it may be time to consider broader changes in the workplace. Advocating for these changes requires courage, but it can lead to improvements that benefit everyone.

Remember, you're not alone. Seeking guidance from mentors or mediators can provide fresh perspectives and strategies. A third party can offer neutrality that's often difficult for those directly involved in the conflict to maintain. Don't hesitate to tap into these resources when needed.

It's important to recognize when a conflict cannot be resolved through direct communication alone. In such cases, using established procedures such as contacting human resources or following formal dispute resolution processes may be necessary. While this avenue may seem formal and daunting, it provides a framework for fair and unbiased resolution.

Mastery of conflict resolution skills is an ongoing journey. It requires self-awareness, patience, and a continuous willingness to learn and adapt. By embedding these practices into your interactions, you enrich not only your own work experience but also contribute positively to the work culture around you. With each resolved conflict, the prospect of a happier, more productive, and balanced work life becomes more attainable.

Chapter 8:
Securing Your Worth: Asking for a Raise

One of the most profound affirmations of our professional value is reflected in our compensation. Yet, the journey to securing a salary that truly matches our worth is often riddled with complex emotions and strategic considerations. When it's time to stride into the negotiation arena, it's essential to prepare a compelling case that underscores your achievements and contributions. Ground your evidence in quantifiable success, such as completed projects, exceeded targets, or streamlined processes that have had a significant impact on the team and the company at large. Preparation, anchored in self-awareness and the acknowledgment of your accomplishments, fortifies your confidence, allowing you to articulate your case not just logically, but with a deserved sense of pride too.

Timing and presentation are pivotal in this delicate dance of negotiation. Concurrent with identifying a moment that's ripe for discussion—perhaps after the successful close of a major deal or the end of a fiscal quarter—comes the nuanced choreography of how you present your case. Approach this conversation with a mindset of collaboration, viewing your manager not as an adversary to conquer, but as a partner in your career progression. Craft your narrative to not only illustrate past triumphs, but to also shine light on your future potential and eagerness to continue contributing to your organization's success. This transforms the dialogue into a forward-looking exploration of mutual growth rather than a retrospective examination.

In the flux of conversations about one's value and worth, the reality of encountering rejection looms heavily. Handling rejection positively is not only vital to maintaining professional relationships; it's a testament to your resilience and adaptability. If the first attempt doesn't swing the pendulum in your favor, inviting feedback can be instrumental. Inquire about specific goals and skills that you can aim for to be considered for a raise in the future. See this moment not as a full stop but as a comma, pausing to regroup and plan for the next step in your career advancement. By maintaining an open mindset and viewing feedback as an opportunity to refine your professional pathway, you're setting the stage for future successes and, eventually, securing your worth.

Preparing Your Case for a raise requires a blend of introspection, strategy, and presentation—it's about more than simply asking for more money. It's a nuanced endeavor that can significantly impact your happiness and work-life balance.

To start, you must dive deep into your achievements. Look back at your time with the company and identify specific instances where your contributions have made a tangible difference. This involves more than a mere list of duties fulfilled; it requires a reflection on instances where you went above and beyond, occasions where you innovated, or times when you played a crucial role in a project's success.

Documenting your success is part of making your case. Don't just rely on your memory; gather evidence. This could be in the form of emails praising your work, statistics showing your productivity, or any accolades you've received. Having a detailed dossier of your successes will not only bolster your case but also boost your confidence when presenting it.

Understanding the company's compensation practices is also key. Research what the market rate is for your role, taking into account your experience and geographical location. Companies often have salary bands or grades; see if this information is available to you via HR or an internal company database. Being informed about where you stand relative to others can be powerful leverage in your negotiations.

Next, consider timing. It's strategic to align your request with the company's budgeting cycle or after the successful completion of a significant project. Sometimes, it's also about sensing the atmosphere in your workplace. Is the company thriving, or are there talks of budget cuts? Your timing should be sensitive to these larger organizational contexts.

In preparing your case, also think about how your role might evolve. If you're seeking more than just a salary increment, such as an upgraded title or additional responsibilities, outline how these changes would benefit both you and the organization. It's important to show that you're thinking of your growth in a way that aligns with the company's future.

Reflect on what motivates you beyond the paycheck. While money is a significant factor, being happy at work often encompasses feeling challenged, valued, and part of something bigger. If these elements are part of your motivation for a raise, articulate them clearly. It shows that you're invested in your job for the right reasons.

Dealing with potential counters is another crucial step. Anticipate what objections or questions your manager might have to your request and prepare reasoned responses. This doesn't just apply to queries over your performance, but also possible budgetary constraints that the company may be facing.

Practicing your pitch is as important as the preparation. Rehearse how you'll articulate your points, keeping your tone confident but not confrontational. Practicing can sharpen your presentation and make you feel more at ease during the actual conversation.

Consider also the human aspect. Managers are not just gatekeepers to a higher salary; they're people who appreciate respect and understanding. Your approach should be as much about building or maintaining a positive relationship as it is about securing a raise.

If you have mentors or trusted colleagues, seek their feedback on your case. They can offer valuable insights, highlight areas you may have overlooked, and even help role-play the negotiation to prepare you for different scenarios.

Keep in mind that patience plays a role in these discussions. Even with a strong case, you may need to negotiate over time. It's vital to stay resilient and maintain your productivity and work quality throughout this process.

During your preparation, also think beyond the immediate goal. Whether or not your request is granted, consider what this process teaches you about your job and your value to the company. Understanding your worth can empower you even if the answer is initially "no".

Last but not least, be prepared for a range of outcomes. If the answer is positive, know exactly what will satisfy you in terms of numbers and job conditions. If the outcome is not what you hoped for, be ready to discuss alternative forms of compensation like additional vacation days, flexible work hours, or professional development opportunities.

Remember, preparing your case for a raise isn't just about improving your financial situation; it's a strategic move towards greater work satisfaction and balance. By meticulously organizing your achievements, understanding your worth, timing your request skillfully, and communicating effectively, you can approach this challenge with confidence.

Timing and Presentation In the dynamic dance of communication, especially when seeking a raise, the when, the how, and the delivery can dramatically tip the scales in your favor—or potentially against it. The carefully crafted request, brought forth at the opportune moment and presented with genuine conviction, holds the power to open doors that lead to well-deserved recognition and reward. This section explores how to identify that golden window of opportunity to make your case, and to do so with a style and grace that strengthens your position.

Timing is more than just a concept; it's the heartbeat of opportunity. To tap into its rhythm, start by observing the ebb and flow of your workplace. Be it the fiscal cycle or the mood pendulum swinging through the office corridors, pinpointing a time when the company is celebrating its wins or basking in the glow of success could offer a more receptive audience for your request. Conversely, raising the subject of a salary increase amidst budget cuts or organizational setbacks may not just be ill-timed, but might also be seen as tone-deaf to the larger context at hand.

The art of presentation begins the moment you decide to ask for a raise, way before you actually vocalize it. It entails the meticulous construction of your case, shaped not only by your achievements and contributions but also by the value you foresee yourself providing in the future. Your communication should be crafted like a tapestry, weaving together a story that resonates with your audience—be that your manager, a team lead, or the HR department. Aim not only to inform but to inspire belief in your worth.

Body language speaks volumes and often conveys more sincerity than words alone. As you prepare, practice your pitch while being mindful of maintaining an open, confident posture. Making eye contact and using affirmative gestures can help to cement your conviction, showcasing a self-assured professional who knows their value. Imagine yourself not just as an employee requesting more but as an equal partner engaging in a transaction beneficial to both parties involved. This perspective shift can transform your approach from one of hesitancy to one of partnership.

Clarity and conciseness should reign supreme in your pitch. The ability to express your request in a straightforward, yet compelling manner reflects both preparation and respect for the time of the person you are addressing. Ground your arguments in fact, sustained by concrete examples of your work, but avoid wandering into unnecessary detail that clouds the main message of your ask.

An principles of mutual respect should underline your presentation. Approaching the conversation with an adversarial "me against them" stance can set the tone for opposition rather than cooperation. Instead, acknowledge the contributions of your team, the pressures and challenges leadership may face, and position your request as one piece in the puzzle of the company's overall success.

Ironically, in the context of timing, patience is a silent player. After making your case, give the decision-makers the time they need to consider your request. Bombarding them with follow-ups or expressing impatience can sour the process. Instead, discern the proper intervals for check-ins, balancing your eagerness with respect for their decision-making process.

One of the critical components of presentation is preparation for pushback. Anticipate possible objections and prepare reasoned, evidence-based responses. It's not uncommon for initial requests to be met with some form of resistance—being prepared to navigate these conversations is a testament to your foresight and investment in the outcome.

Consideration for the other person's perspective is also vital. Understand that approval for a raise isn't always a simple yes or no decision. Budget constraints, equity among team members, and timing from a fiscal standpoint can all play into the response you receive. By demonstrating empathy and understanding of these factors, you build goodwill even as you advocate for yourself.

Emotional intelligence can be your ally in reading the subtext of a conversation. Stay attuned not just to what is being said but how it's being said. The tone, the pauses, the choice of words—all provide cues that can help you gauge the direction and flow of the dialogue, allowing you to adjust your approach in real time.

In addition to the spoken word, your written materials should be equally polished. Whether it's a summary e-mail outlining your accomplishments, a brief but impactful presentation deck, or supporting documentation, these materials should echo the professionalism of your pitch, demonstrating a commitment to detail and quality in all aspects of your work.

Remember that the outcome of your request for a raise is not solely within your control, but how you handle the response is. If the answer is positive, express gratitude and discuss next steps. If it's negative, seek to understand the rationale, and ask for constructive feedback or possible alternatives. This isn't just about accepting a decision passively; it's about maintaining a position of proactive engagement.

A graceful exit is as pivotal as a powerful entrance. Whether or not you achieve the desired raise, conclude your discussions with appreciation for the time and consideration given to your request. This cements you as a professional who maintains composure and courtesy, regardless of the outcome.

Reflect on the experience as a growth opportunity. Irrespective of the result, each attempt at negotiation hones your skills and prepares you for future conversations. View these engagements not just as transactions but as part of a larger journey of professional development and self-advocacy.

Essentially, the decision to seek a raise is a step towards asserting your value within the organization. The careful orchestration of timing and presentation isn't simply about strategy; it's a demonstration of self-respect, understanding of organizational dynamics, and mastery of the art of communication—skills that will stand you in good stead not just in this instance, but throughout your career.

Handling Rejection Positively

The journey toward securing a raise is fraught with challenges, and one that may arise is rejection. The sting of being turned down, despite careful preparation and timing, can be a formidable test of resilience. Yet, it's in these moments, in the silent aftermath of a 'no,' that there lies a profound opportunity for growth and self-reflection.

Rejection, in its essence, is not a full stop but a comma in the narrative of our professional lives. It's imperative to view it not as a reflection of one's worth, but as a navigational aid that points us toward new paths for development. The potency of this experience hinges on maintaining perspective. When a request for a raise is met with rejection, it's essential to detach our personal value from the outcome; our abilities are not diminished by this single event.

Handling rejection with grace begins with acknowledging feelings of disappointment without letting them cloud our self-assessment. By affording ourselves a moment to process these emotions, we allow clarity to emerge. This clarity is pivotal, as it guides our next steps with purpose rather than impulse.

In the wake of rejection, seeking constructive feedback becomes invaluable. Engaging in a dialogue with a supervisor about the factors that led to the decision can provide insights that are both enlightening and actionable. This feedback is a gift, one that can reshape your approach, refine your skills, and strengthen future requests.

It's also beneficial to revisit your preparation process. Did you articulate your value compellingly? Was your timing optimal? Re-examining your strategy can show you where you might need to bolster your case or adjust your approach. Thus, the experience of being denied a raise can serve as a catalyst for recalibration and growth.

Yet, feedback and self-reflection should also be balanced with a broader view of success. Opportunities for advancement and compensation aren't limited to singular occasions; they are abundant. Cultivating patience and tenacity is crucial for long-term success and maintains our drive in the face of setbacks.

A healthy mindset also involves setting aside time to care for oneself. Indulgence in self-care practices after a rejection is not a sign of defeat, but a strategic retreat that allows you to recharge and build resilience. Whether through exercise, relaxation techniques, or engaging in hobbies, it's vital to replenish your energy stores.

Moreover, fostering a supportive network at work can provide both a sounding board and a source of encouragement. Colleagues and mentors who have experienced similar challenges can offer wisdom and empathetic understanding that contextualize our experience within a shared human narrative.

Rejection can also be reframed as a reminder of your courage; the very act of asking for a raise is commendable. It demonstrates initiative, self-advocacy, and a commitment to your professional advancement. Every attempt, regardless of outcome, builds confidence and hones negotiation skills.

One must not overlook the power of adaptability. In the dynamic landscape of the workplace, aligning oneself with the evolution of roles and responsibilities can uncover alternative avenues for recognition and reward. Staying attuned to these shifts can unlock doors that were previously unseen.

Finally, it's important to recognize that sometimes a rejection can be serendipitous. It can prompt you to evaluate your career path and consider whether your current environment aligns with your aspirations. Moments of rejection may spur the search for new professional realms where your talents are met with the appreciation—and compensation—they deserve.

While rejection is undoubtedly challenging, it can become a profound teacher. Each 'no' refines your strategies, hones your resilience, and deepens your understanding of the workplace dynamics. By facing rejection with positivity and proactive responses, you don't just cope; you transform what could be a paralyzing obstacle into a stepping stone toward future success.

As we navigate the undulations of rejection, it's the wisdom we accrue and the resilience we build that lay the foundation for the eventual 'yes' that will come. Our worth, undeterred by a momentary set-back, is validated not by external affirmation but by the tenacity and self-compassion with which we move forward.

Embracing this approach to handling rejection positively is not only conducive to a happier work experience but also to an improved sense of self-worth and well-being beyond the office walls. It paves the way for a career marked by persistent growth, joy in the face of adversity, and an enduring balance between work and life.

Chapter 9: Advocating for Workplace Accommodations

The pursuit of happiness, productivity, and balance in the workplace often hinges on the environment we cultivate and the accommodations we secure to support our unique needs. In this chapter, we delve into the essential strategies for advocating for workplace accommodations, creating a space where individual needs are not just recognized, but actively accommodated. Whether it stems from a physical disability, a mental health consideration, or a learning difference, the right accommodations are vital to providing a level playing field for all employees.

Understanding one's rights forms the bedrock of effective advocacy. Every employee should be equipped with a foundational knowledge of the legal protections and inclusive policies that uphold their entitlement to accommodations, such as the Americans with Disabilities Act (ADA). From there, crafting a clear and confident approach becomes invaluable. This isn't merely about asking for aid; it's a conversation about optimizing one's ability to contribute, collaborate, and thrive within the team. Articulating one's needs with clarity, without apology, invites an openness from management to explore and implement targeted solutions. Remember, these requests reflect an employee's commitment to their work and their well-being – both of which are in the best interest of the employer.

The art of negotiation comes into play when considering the practicalities of the requested accommodations. Successful negotiation is built upon mutual understanding and respect, requiring both the employee and employer to navigate towards a consensus that acknowledges the value of the accommodation while balancing it against the company's capabilities and resources. Strategies such as proposing trial periods, providing evidence-based research on the benefits of the requested adjustments, and demonstrating flexibility can all foster a more receptive and collaborative negotiation process. When done right, advocating for workplace accommodations strengthens the individual's ability to be their most productive self and can even spark broader positive changes in the organization's commitment to an accessible and inclusive work environment.

Understanding Your Rights

In the journey to harmonize the sometimes discordant melody of work life and personal contentment, it's crucial to understand the rights you have within your workplace. Knowing these can serve as the compass that guides you through a fog of uncertainties, allowing you to advocate for your well-being effectively. The patchwork of legislation, corporate policies, and ethical norms carve out an employee's sanctuary within the professional environment. Here, we'll outline those sanctuaries and arm you with the knowledge to protect and advance your interests.

It's essential to recognize that each country—and often each region within that country—has its set of labor laws. These statutes define your work hours, break times, compensation, and protection against unlawful employment practices. In the U.S., for instance, the Fair Labor Standards Act (FLSA) may not promise you serenity at sunset, but it does assure minimum wage and overtime pay, anchoring your financial security.

Moreover, discrimination in the workplace is not just a matter of moral disgrace but also legal concern. Laws such as the Equal Employment Opportunity Commission (EEOC) enforce the federal prohibition against job discrimination. Consider these your shield against the arrows of bias based on age, sex, color, religion, national origin, disability, or genetic information.

The right to a safe work environment might seem as natural as breathing, yet it's written into law for a reason. Agencies like the Occupational Safety and Health

Administration (OSHA) set and enforce standards to maintain your physical wellbeing at work, turning the tide against hazardous neglect and ensuring that you're not compromising your health for a paycheck.

In matters of privacy, most jurisdictions will ensure your personal information is safeguarded. Your employer must walk the tightrope between managing its workforce and respecting the confidentiality of your personal and medical information. The Health Insurance Portability and Accountability Act (HIPAA) is one such law that binds employers from untethering your privacy rights.

The Family and Medical Leave Act (FMLA) recognizes that employees are not mere cogs in the machine but individuals with lives that sometimes demand their undivided attention. It ensures that for specified family and medical reasons, you can take unpaid, job-protected leave, with the continuation of group health insurance coverage under the same terms and conditions as if you had not taken leave.

Balancing work and family life can sometimes feel like masterfully playing a grand piano while juggling responsibilities; the Pregnancy Discrimination Act ensures that women don't face employment discrimination due to pregnancy, childbirth, or related medical conditions. Accommodations must be made, allowing for the crescendo of family life without the diminuendo of career progression.

Furthermore, as the world increasingly recognizes the spectrum of abilities, the Americans with Disabilities Act (ADA) prohibits discrimination against individuals with disabilities in all areas of public life. It stands as a testament to inclusivity, making sure that all have access to the symphony of opportunities that work provides.

The right to report discriminatory or unsafe work conditions is also your amulet. Whistleblower protection laws prevent retaliation against employees who sound the horn against employer violations. You should be able to sing out truths without fear of having your voice stifled.

For those times when the professional world's noise overwhelms, workers' compensation laws provide restitution. If injury or illness orchestrates itself from the conduct of your employment, there are measures in place to cover your medical treatments and partially compensate for your lost wages. It's a harmony of legal provisions that cater to the unfortunate eventualities.

Additionally, remember that your employment contract can augment your rights with its own set of clauses, sometimes extending protections beyond the bare bones of the law. Think of it as a concerto's soloist—distinctly improving upon the overall harmony, giving you more room to breathe and assert your needs.

Let's not forget the budding movement for mental health awareness in the workplace. While not always enshrined into hard law, many companies are now adopting policies that recognize and address stress, anxiety, and other mental health challenges. These policies act as preventative medicine, intending to circumvent workplace stressors before they turn into full-blown crises.

When it comes to understanding your rights, knowledge is the prelude to empowerment. Keep in mind that staying informed of updates and changes in legislation is essential in performing to the best of your ability. Changes in laws and policies can happen swiftly, but with the right information, you're prepared to adjust accordingly.

If ever you find your rights being violated, the path of remedy includes reporting the issue through the appropriate internal channels, or going a step further and seeking the guidance of legal experts or labor unions, if available. Just as a conductor leads an orchestra to ensure each instrument is in harmony, such advisors can help lead your cause toward resolution.

It's the community of colleagues, the shared camaraderie, and support networks that can be your greatest allies in understanding and exercising your rights. There's strength in numbers, and often, change is most effective when driven by a collective. A solo may command a powerful moment, but the chorus can move the entire performance.

Comprehending your workplace rights isn't just about building defenses; it's about shaping an environment where you can thrive. Each article of law and line in policy plays its part in the grand composition of your work life. By understanding your rights, you are tuning your instrument to play the grand symphony of your career to its richest sound.

Effective Communication Strategies are the cornerstone of advocating successfully for workplace accommodations. Communication is not merely about conveying a message but about ensuring it is received and understood as intended. At work, expressing needs and rights while maintaining professional relationships requires a blend of clarity, empathy, and strategic planning.

It's essential to be clear and concise. When you know the accommodations you need, lay them out in simple terms. Explain how these changes can benefit not just you but the organization. By making a direct connection between your needs and increased productivity or decreased stress, you're more likely to gain your employer's support.

Listening is just as important as speaking. Engage in active listening to understand the concerns and limitations your employer may have. Acknowledge these concerns and be prepared to offer solutions or come to a compromise. This two-way discourse cements the idea that accommodations are a collaborative effort.

Timing also plays a pivotal role in your approach. Choose a moment to discuss your needs when you're unlikely to be interrupted, and the individual you're speaking with can give you their full attention. A rushed conversation can lead to misunderstandings or undervaluing of your request.

A well-crafted narrative can be a powerful tool. Share a personal story that highlights the challenges you're facing without accommodations. This human element can foster understanding and make the need for adaptations more tangible to decision-makers.

Non-verbal cues are part of the communication package. Your body language, eye contact, and tone convey confidence and sincerity. These subtleties can significantly influence the receptivity of your message, reinforcing your spoken words.

Emotional intelligence is vital. While it's important to be assertive, balance it with tact and respect for the organizational culture. Understanding the emotional undercurrents can help navigate a path that is considerate of all parties' feelings and perspectives.

Drafting a written request can also be beneficial. This allows for careful choice of words and provides a reference for your employer. It keeps the discourse professional and means you're less likely to leave out important details in the moment.

Practice makes perfect. Rehearse your talking points to make the actual conversation smoother. Anticipate potential questions and prepare your responses to them, which will help reduce anxiety and increase coherence during the discussion.

Utilize affirmative language. Frame your needs positively, focusing on what can be done rather than what can't. Positivity has persuasive power, encouraging solution-oriented thinking and cooperation.

It can also be effective to demonstrate your commitment to your work. Highlight your past contributions and reiterate your desire to continue performing at a high level. This shows that your request for accommodations comes from a place of wanting to succeed, not just personal convenience.

Further, be specific about the accommodations you're seeking. Vague requests can lead to vague responses. If you need specific software, a flexible schedule, or ergonomic furniture, state it explicitly. Specifics allow for a clear assessment and discussion regarding implementation.

If an immediate agreement isn't reached, suggest a trial period for the accommodations. This reduces risk for the employer and provides tangible evidence of the accommodation's effectiveness.

Remember that negotiation may be necessary. Stay open to suggestions that may achieve the same result through different means. Flexibility demonstrates that you're working with the organization, rather than making demands of it.

Document all communications related to your accommodation requests. This is not only for your records but also serves as a professional way to summarize discussions and agreed-upon action steps, ensuring that both you and your employer have clear expectations and understandings.

Effective communication for advocating workplace accommodations requires a sensitive and considered approach. It's not just about getting your point across; it's about building a bridge of understanding with your employer that can support the modifications needed to facilitate your happiness, productivity, and well-being at work. By tailoring your communication strategy with the tips mentioned, you help pave the way for an accommodating work environment that respects individual needs and upholds the collective harmony of the workplace.

Negotiating for Your Needs Conversations around workplace accommodations are not merely transactional;

they're deeply rooted in understanding and articulating your unique needs while aligning them with the objectives of the organization. When you find yourself requiring certain adjustments or resources to maximize your work potential, it becomes essential to approach these negotiations with a strategic and empathetic mindset.

Navigating requests for accommodations involves a blend of self-awareness and diplomacy. Consider first your internal compass: what exactly do you need? Whether it's related to an ergonomic desk setup to alleviate physical strain, flextime to manage family commitments, or other adjustments that promote well-being, defining your needs in concrete terms is the first critical step.

Once you've identified your needs, the next phase is to gather evidence in support of your request. This might include medical records, research highlighting the benefits of specific accommodations, or a written statement outlining the ways in which the accommodation would enhance your productivity. Tangible evidence strengthens your case, demonstrating foresight and preparation.

Preparation also involves anticipating potential objections. Go into the negotiation with a clear understanding of possible resistance points and have a plan to address them. Emphasizing the mutual benefits — how your effectiveness in your role is ultimately good for the team and organization — can shift the conversation from a request for special treatment to a discussion on optimizing workforce efficiency.

Communication here is an art. It's about striking a balance between assertiveness and empathy. While you should be firm in conveying the importance of your needs, it's equally crucial to listen to the concerns or constraints the employer may have. Active listening and a willingness to understand the perspective of your employer can create an atmosphere of cooperation, rather than conflict.

Timing is another crucial element to consider. Choose a moment to discuss accommodations when you are not under stress from deadlines or other pressures. A calm, collected approach will convey that you've thought the situation through, rather than acting out of immediate frustration or need.

It's possible your initial request may not be fully granted. In such cases, flexibility is key. Be open to alternatives or phases of implementation that might be more acceptable to your employer. Suggest starting with a pilot period for the accommodation, allowing for adjustments and proving its efficacy without a long-term commitment initially.

Negotiations can also involve compromise. Be prepared to give and take. You might have to adjust your expectations and consider less-than-ideal solutions that still move in the direction of your needs. It's essential not to view compromise as defeat, but as a step towards a mutually beneficial resolution.

If negotiations reach a standstill, it might be helpful to seek the involvement of a third party, such as a human resources representative or a workplace mediator. This individual can assist in finding a middle ground and ensure that the conversation stays on track toward a resolution.

Documentation is your ally. Keep a thorough record of all communications and agreements regarding the negotiation process. This clarifies any outcomes and provides a reference should there be any future disputes or need for reevaluation.

While negotiating for your needs, it's vital to maintain a professional demeanor. Avoid letting emotions steer the conversation; stay focused on the facts and the desired outcome. By keeping the discussion respectful and solution-oriented, you foster a positive environment for negotiation.

Remember that negotiation is an ongoing process, not a one-time event. Be prepared for continuous dialogue, especially if accommodations need refining over time. Frequent check-ins with your employer will demonstrate your commitment to finding workable solutions and maintaining open communication.

In some instances, despite best efforts, negotiations may not yield the desired outcomes. If you reach this point, it may be necessary to reassess your position within the company. Weighing the importance of certain accommodations against your overall career goals can provide clarity on your next steps — whether that's seeking alternative solutions or considering a different work environment more conducive to your needs.

Throughout the process, strive to maintain a clear understanding of your rights. While employers are generally required to provide reasonable accommodations, knowing the specifics of legal protections relevant to your situation, such as those within the Americans with Disabilities Act (if applicable), can empower you in discussions and negotiations.

No matter the outcome, view each negotiation as a learning experience. It hones your skills in communication, compromise, and self-advocacy — all of which are invaluable in the professional world. By approaching the negotiation process with clarity, preparation, and resilience, you not only advocate for a better work situation but also contribute to building a more inclusive and understanding workplace culture.

Chapter 10: Bringing Ideas to the Forefront

In our journey toward achieving happiness at work, it's essential not just to navigate stressors or maintain productivity, but also to ensure that our voices are heard—that our ideas make the jump from fleeting thoughts to impactful contributions. Whether it's a groundbreaking project proposal, a workflow enhancement, or a creative solution to a pressing issue, the art of bringing ideas to the forefront is central to personal fulfillment and professional advancement. Crafting a persuasive pitch isn't merely about laying out facts but weaving a narrative that compels your audience to listen, understand, and act.

But what happens when our ideas meet resistance? Overcoming objections is an inevitable part of the process. It's not just a test of the idea itself but of resilience and adaptability. The key is not to view objections as roadblocks but as opportunities to refine your proposition. Engaging with skeptics and addressing their concerns head-on can strengthen your case and build broader support. It also fosters a culture of openness and constructive feedback, where ideas are polished through collaboration rather than rejected by confrontation.

Rallying support for your idea requires more than just a robust argument. It's about connecting with people on a deeper level—understanding their motivations, anticipating their needs, and articulating how your idea can serve the greater good. This means stepping into the shoes of your colleagues, your supervisors, and the organization at large. It's finding that common thread that links individual aspirations to collective goals, making your idea everyone's mission.

At its core, bringing ideas to the forefront is about leadership. But not the kind that is conferred by titles or positions. It's a leadership rooted in authenticity, empathy, and the courage to challenge the status quo. It's about being the spark that ignites innovation and the glue that binds a team toward a shared vision. And as you embark on this process, remember that every groundbreaking change once started as a mere suggestion, a "what if" whispered in the shadows of doubt. Your idea could be the next catalyst for transformation, but only if you dare to bring it into the light.

So, as we move forward, let's embrace the possibilities that lie not just in refining our work habits or creating balance but in actively shaping the environments we inhabit. Because ultimately, happiness at work isn't just about surviving; it's about thriving—leveraging our creativity, our passion, and our voices to craft a reality that resonates with who we are and what we believe in. Let's not just be part of the conversation. Let's lead it.

Crafting a Persuasive Pitch As we navigate the complexities of the workplace, it becomes essential to articulate our ideas in ways that resonate, influencing outcomes positively. Crafted correctly, a persuasive pitch can be the catalyst for change, opening doors and creating opportunities that align with our aspirations for happiness, productivity, and work-life balance. Herein lies the art of turning visions into shared ambitions, an endeavor that demands clarity, empathy, and strategic execution.

Understanding your audience is paramount. Each individual you're pitching to comes with their own set of priorities, fears, and motivations. A pitch that fails to consider these elements is akin to navigating a ship without a compass. Begin by asking yourself what truly matters to them. Is it increased productivity, reduced costs, or perhaps fostering a more positive workplace environment? Tapping into these motivations can make your pitch compelling and hard to ignore.

Clarity is your ally. An idea, no matter how groundbreaking, loses its luster if muddled in complexity. Simplicity in communication does not equate to insignificance; rather, it signifies respect for the audience's time and an understanding of the essence of your proposition. Break down your idea into digestible pieces, ensuring that your vision is communicated with both precision and passion.

The power of storytelling cannot be underestimated. People are moved by narrative - stories that stir emotions and paint vivid pictures in our minds. When crafting your pitch, weave a narrative that showcases not just the what, but the why and how. Highlight real or hypothetical scenarios where your idea could have a tangible, positive impact. This approach not only engages your audience but also makes your idea more relatable and memorable.

Empathy plays a critical role. Putting yourself in the shoes of your audience allows you to foresee potential objections and address them proactively. Acknowledge the challenges and uncertainties your idea might pose, and offer well-considered solutions. This demonstrates not only thorough preparation but also a commitment to collaboration and problem-solving.

Anticipate objections, and arm yourself with data and evidence. In the face of skepticism, anecdotal evidence can only take you so far. Arm yourself with research, case studies, and statistics that support your idea. Accurate data presented at the right moment can turn the tide, transforming doubt into confidence.

Timing is everything. Even the most persuasive pitch can falter if presented at an inopportune moment. Gauge the mood, workload, and current concerns of your audience. Sometimes, waiting for a more receptive moment or a trigger event can significantly increase your chances of success.

Confidence is key, but humility is your secret weapon. Approach your pitch with confidence, showcasing your belief in the idea. Yet, remain open to feedback. Showing that you value the opinions and expertise of your audience fosters an environment of mutual respect and collaboration.

Less is often more. The temptation to share every facet of your idea can be overwhelming. However, an overloaded pitch can distract and even disengage your audience. Focus on the core of your idea, the benefits, and its potential impact. Leave room for questions; this engagement can provide valuable insights into the concerns or interests of your audience.

Follow-up is as important as the pitch itself. After you've shared your idea, don't leave the conversation hanging. Provide additional information if requested, offer to address any concerns in more detail, and express your gratitude for the opportunity to present. This persistent, yet respectful, follow-up can keep your idea on their radar.

Practice makes perfect. Prior to delivering your pitch, rehearse it several times. Familiarity with your material allows you to speak more naturally and adjust on the fly if necessary. Whether it's in front of a mirror, with a trusted colleague, or through a video recording, practicing your delivery can significantly improve your performance.

Embrace the art of visual storytelling. When appropriate, supplement your pitch with visuals - charts, graphs, images that encapsulate your idea's essence. Visual aids can not only make your pitch more engaging but also help clarify complex ideas, making them accessible to a wider audience.

Mind your body language. Non-verbal cues often speak louder than words. Maintain eye contact, stand confidently, and use gestures that reinforce your message. These seemingly minor details can greatly enhance the effectiveness of your communication, making your pitch more persuasive.

Remember that a persuasive pitch is not just about achieving a personal goal. It's about fostering positive change, whether it's enhancing workplace well-being, productivity, or achieving a better work-life balance. Your pitch, at its core, should reflect a deep-seated desire to contribute to a better work environment for everyone involved.

Crafting a persuasive pitch is a meticulous art that blends empathy, strategic thinking, and effective communication. By approaching it with the right mindset, preparation, and respect for your audience, you can turn your ideas into catalysts for meaningful change. Remember, the goal is not just to persuade but to inspire action that aligns with shared values and objectives for a happier, more balanced workplace experience.

Overcoming Objections In the journey of bringing ideas to the forefront, one of the most formidable challenges you'll face is overcoming objections. Whether these come from colleagues, supervisors, or even within yourself, the ability to navigate and dismantle these objections is crucial for progress. The art of persuasion isn't just about pushing forward; it's as much about listening, understanding, and addressing concerns in a constructive manner. This section is dedicated to equipping you with strategies to handle objections effectively, ensuring your ideas get the consideration they deserve.

The first step in overcoming objections is to anticipate them. Before you present your idea, take a moment to step into the shoes of your audience. What concerns might they have? How does your proposal impact their workload, resources, or goals? By anticipating these concerns, you can prepare responses that address them proactively. For instance, if your idea involves a new project that requires additional manpower, consider suggesting a phased approach that mitigates the impact on current resources.

Listening is just as important as speaking when you're dealing with objections. Often, people just want to know that their concerns are acknowledged. When you're presented with an objection, resist the urge to respond immediately. Instead, listen attentively, validate the concern ("I understand why that's a worry..."), and then respond calmly. This approach not only shows respect but also gives you time to formulate a thoughtful answer.

Questions are a powerful tool in your arsenal. Rather than defending your idea defensively, ask questions that guide your audience to find the answer themselves. For example, if the objection is about the feasibility of a new project, ask, "What would make it feasible for us?" This approach encourages collaborative problem-solving and increases the chances of your idea being accepted.

Flexibility is key. Sometimes, despite your best efforts, you'll need to adjust your idea. Being too rigid can be a barrier to progress. Show your audience that you're open to feedback and willing to incorporate their suggestions. This doesn't mean compromising on the core of your idea but finding a middle ground where everyone's needs are met.

Focus on the benefits. When addressing objections, highlight the benefits of your idea. How does it align with the overall goals of the team or organization? What problem does it solve? By focusing on the benefits, you shift the conversation from a critique of the idea to a discussion about its potential impact.

Use evidence and data to support your argument. Objections are often based on emotions or assumptions. By providing data and evidence, you can counter these with facts. This could include case studies, statistics, or projections that demonstrate the value of your idea.

Illustrate your commitment. Demonstrating your commitment to an idea can be a persuasive tool in overcoming objections. Show that you're not just proposing an idea but are willing to lead its implementation. This reassures others that you've considered the practicalities and are invested in its success.

Addressing the fear of change is often necessary. Many objections stem from a fear of the unknown. Acknowledge this fear and discuss ways to mitigate risk. This could involve a pilot project or phased implementation, allowing for adjustments based on feedback and results.

Build allies. Before presenting your idea to a larger group, discuss it with key individuals who can be your allies. If you can address their objections one-on-one, they can support you when you present to a larger audience. Their endorsement can also help sway others.

Keep it positive. Even when faced with strong opposition, maintain a positive demeanor. Positivity is infectious and can help lower defenses, making it easier to address objections. Avoid getting defensive or negative, as this only raises barriers.

Practice patience. Overcoming objections doesn't happen overnight. It's a process that requires patience and persistence. Don't be discouraged by initial resistance. Instead, view it as an opportunity to refine your idea and build support over time.

Remember, objections aren't just obstacles; they're opportunities for dialogue and improvement. By approaching them with positivity, flexibility, and a willingness to listen, you can transform resistance into support. This not only increases the chances of your idea being adopted but also strengthens your relationships with colleagues and supervisors. After all, the goal isn't merely to get your way, but to find the best way forward together.

Overcoming objections is a critical skill in the workplace. It requires a blend of empathy, strategy, and resilience. By adopting the strategies outlined in this section, you'll be well-equipped to navigate objections and bring your ideas to the forefront. Embrace objections as part of the journey towards innovation and progress, and let them guide you to stronger, more refined proposals that have the potential to transform your workplace.

As we move on, remember that overcoming objections is just one piece of the puzzle. Rallying support for your idea, which we'll cover next, is another crucial step. The journey from conception to implementation is filled with challenges, but with the right approach, each obstacle is a stepping stone to success.

Rallying Support for Your Idea Continuing from our exploration into bringing innovative ideas to the forefront, garnering support within your work environment is a crucial next step. The vitality of this stage can't be overstressed. It's where your project transitions from concept to potential reality. Imagine your idea as a spark. Alone, it's bright but fleeting. With the right support, it turns into a beacon that guides your team or organization forward.

In seeking support, your first ally is clarity. Clearly articulated ideas resonate more strongly with others. When you've delved deep into the intricacies of your idea, it's easy to overlook the importance of conveying it in simple, impactful terms. Remember, not everyone has journeyed through the thought process with you. Start by distilling your idea into a compelling elevator pitch. This should succinctly answer the 'what', 'why', and 'how' of your proposition in a manner that's easily digestible.

Building on clarity, the next vital step is identifying stakeholders. These are the individuals whose support is imperative. They might be directly impacted by your idea, possess the authority to approve it, or have the skills and resources needed for implementation. Understanding your stakeholders allows you to tailor your approach to each group or individual, meeting them where they're at and addressing their unique interests and concerns.

Engagement is not a one-shot effort. It demands consistency. This means keeping stakeholders updated on progress, setbacks, and pivots. Transparency builds trust, and trust paves the way for continued support. Moreover, engagement is a two-way street. Seek feedback actively and listen genuinely. This doesn't mean bending your idea to fit every whim but being open to constructive suggestions that could refine and strengthen your proposal.

Now, let's talk about leveraging success stories. If your idea or elements of it have been successfully executed elsewhere, share these examples as evidence of its viability. Success stories serve as powerful testimonials to the efficacy and potential impact of your proposition. They can significantly reduce perceived risks, making stakeholders more comfortable in offering their support.

Emotional appeal is another powerful tool at your disposal. People are often moved by what they feel as much as by what they think. If your idea has a strong human element, highlight this. Whether it's improving work-life balance, enhancing job satisfaction, or reducing stress, relate your idea back to the personal benefits for individuals within the organization. This connection can turn passive listeners into active supporters.

Developing a prototype or a pilot can also help in rallying support. A tangible representation of your idea makes it more concrete. It allows people to see and sometimes even interact with the concept, making it easier for them to understand and get behind it. Even a simple mock-up or a detailed project plan can serve this function, depending on the nature of your idea.

Fostering allies within the organization is also critical. Look for individuals who share your enthusiasm for the idea. They can become champions in their own right, helping to spread the word and sway opinion. This network of support can be invaluable, particularly in overcoming skepticism or resistance.

Anticipate objections and be prepared with responses. It's natural for people to have reservations about new ideas, especially if they disrupt the status quo. Carefully consider potential concerns and craft thoughtful, evidence-backed responses to these. Being prepared shows that you've thought through the idea thoroughly and can increase your credibility.

Persistence is key. Very few ideas are embraced overnight. Prepare yourself for a journey that may require you to repeatedly demonstrate the value of your proposal. This persistence, combined with a clear vision and genuine passion, can eventually sway those who are undecided or resistant.

Networking outside your organization can also provide support. Sometimes, bringing in an external perspective can add weight to your proposal. Whether it's a respected expert in the field, an industry influencer, or a case study from a similar organization, external validation can enhance the credibility of your idea.

Don't underestimate the power of timing. Introducing your idea at the right moment can significantly influence its reception. This could mean aligning with organizational priorities, capitalizing on recent successes, or introducing your idea in a period of relative stability when stakeholders are more open to exploration and innovation.

Remember, rallying support is as much about the people you're engaging with as it is about the idea itself. Paying attention to the human element—listening, empathizing, and responding—can make all the difference in gaining the momentum needed to turn your idea into a reality.

Mobilizing support for your idea requires a blend of strategic planning, interpersonal engagement, and sometimes, a bit of patience. But the fruits of this labor, in the form of a project that improves your workplace or even sets new standards within your industry, can be immensely rewarding. Consider each conversation, each pitch, and each demonstration as stepping stones leading to that ultimate goal.

Rallying support for your idea is an intricate dance of persuasion, persistence, and partnership. It's about convincingly communicating the value of your proposal, harnessing the power of collaboration, and navigating the complexities of organizational dynamics. With the right approach, your idea has the potential not just to take off but to soar, bringing positive change and, importantly, contributing to your happiness, productivity, and work-life balance. It's a journey well worth embarking on.

Chapter 11: Influencing Workplace Policies and Procedures

Stepping into the conversation about altering workplace policies and procedures can feel like navigating a vast and complex labyrinth. Yet, the impact of thoughtful change on our well-being, productivity, and overall happiness at work cannot be overstressed. It starts with identifying areas ripe for improvement—those policies and procedures that, if tweaked, could make significant positive differences in our everyday work life and that of our colleagues. But recognizing these areas is just the starting point. The real challenge lies in championing change in environments that might resist it due to tradition, inertia, or a simple lack of awareness.

Building a compelling case for change demands more than just good intentions. It requires gathering concrete evidence, understanding the intricacies of the existing policies, and, perhaps most crucially, empathy. Crafting your proposal in a way that aligns with the organization's goals while also highlighting the benefits for the workforce can bridge the gap between resistance and acceptance. This approach transforms the conversation from one of critique to one of collaboration, with a focus on mutual gains.

Navigating organizational politics is an art in itself. It's about knowing who the decision-makers are, the influencers who can champion your cause, and the colleagues who will be directly impacted by the change. It's essential to engage in open dialogues, listen actively, and be prepared to adjust your proposals based on feedback. This process isn't just about achieving a specific change; it's also about fostering a culture of openness, where ideas and concerns can be shared freely and constructively.

However, influencing change is not a one-off endeavor. It's an ongoing process of engagement, feedback, and refinement. Success might not come overnight, and setbacks are part of the journey. Yet, persistence pays off. Celebrating small victories and learning from less successful attempts can keep the momentum going. It's about cultivating an environment where positive change is not just welcomed but encouraged—a place where each person feels empowered to contribute to the collective well-being and success of the organization.

Influencing workplace policies and procedures is a pathway laden with challenges but also ripe with rewards.

It's an opportunity to shape an environment that reflects our needs, values, and aspirations. By approaching this task with a blend of strategic thinking, empathy, and resilience, we can make a tangible difference in our workplaces, contributing not just to our happiness and productivity but to fostering a culture of inclusivity and innovation.

Identifying Areas for Improvement is pivotal in sculpting a workplace that not only breeds productivity but also ensures the well-being of its contributors. Every organization, no matter its accolades or achievements, has room for enhancement. The journey towards recognizing these areas can be intricate, involving serious introspection and observation.

We must understand that improvement starts with acknowledging the current state of affairs. It's akin to navigating through a dense forest; one needs to know where they stand before plotting a course. In the context of a workplace, this could mean assessing the environment, the culture, the processes, and the outcomes. Are there elements that hinder productivity or employee satisfaction? Sometimes, it's the small pebbles, not just the boulders, that trip us up.

Listening plays a critical role here. Feedback from employees, both solicited and unsolicited, provides invaluable insights into what's working and what's not. It's essential to create a culture where feedback is not just welcomed but sought after. This open communication paves the way for identifying specific areas needing improvement. Remember, the goal isn't to assign blame but to find opportunities for growth and enhancement.

Moreover, the analysis of performance metrics cannot be overstated. They offer an objective lens through which the effectiveness of various strategies and processes can be evaluated. Are there targets being consistently missed? Are there recurring complaints in certain departments? Numbers and data often highlight issues that might be overlooked in the day-to-day hustle.

Another crucial aspect is comparing your organization's practices with industry standards or benchmarks. This comparison can shed light on discrepancies and gaps in processes or policies. Perhaps there's a more efficient system or tool being utilized elsewhere that could drastically improve your operations.

Engaging with the frontline employees and understanding their daily hurdles can illuminate areas ripe for improvement. These are the individuals who interact with the products, services, and customers directly; their hands-on experience is gold dust for uncovering inefficiencies or areas of friction.

Then, there's the leadership lens. Leadership styles and dynamics have a profound influence on the workplace atmosphere and efficiency. Leaders must be open to introspection and critique as well. Is there a leadership approach that's stifling creativity or innovation? Are there communication gaps creating unnecessary obstacles?

Technology audit is another angle from which to approach this exploration. In an era driven by digital transformation, staying updated with the latest tools and platforms is essential. Perhaps there are technological solutions available that could automate mundane tasks or streamline complex processes, thereby freeing up time for more strategic activities.

Moreover, evaluating the company's learning and development initiatives can provide insights into areas of improvement. Are employees being equipped with the skills required to excel in their roles and adapt to future changes? An organization that invests in its people's growth fosters a culture of continuous improvement and innovation.

Cultural evaluation too cannot be ignored. A workplace culture that doesn't align with contemporary values of diversity, equity, and inclusion may need a significant overhaul. The culture within an organization impacts employee engagement, retention, and even customer perceptions.

Furthermore, reconsider the channels and methods of internal communication. Miscommunications or information silos can derail even the most well-intentioned strategies. Streamlining communication can often lead to quick wins in improving productivity and morale.

Similarly, scrutinizing the work environment itself – the physical and virtual spaces – can reveal improvements that foster better focus, collaboration, and well-being. Sometimes, a re-arrangement of the workspace or an upgrade to more collaborative tools can spark a significant shift in productivity and employee satisfaction.

An organization must also routinely reassess its goals and objectives to ensure they remain relevant and challenging. The business world is dynamic, and a failure to adapt goals accordingly can leave a company lagging behind its competitors. Are the current objectives pushing the organization towards growth and innovation?

Engaging in regular strategic reviews can help keep the organization agile and responsive. It's about continuously asking, "What can we do better?" and not shying away from the sometimes uncomfortable answers. It's about embracing change – not as a threat but as an opportunity for development and learning.

Identifying areas for improvement is a comprehensive exercise that stretches across all facets of an organization. It requires a collective effort, a willingness to listen, and a commitment to act. Improvement is not a destination but a journey – one that, when embraced, can lead to a workplace that not only achieves its goals but also supports the well-being and growth of its people.

Building a Compelling Case for Change Change within any organization is both an opportunity and a challenge. It's a journey embarked upon not just by leaders but by every individual within the structure. Crafting a compelling case for this change, especially when aiming to influence workplace policies and procedures, requires an insightful blend of strategy, empathy, and clear communication. This chapter guides you through the nuances of bringing about meaningful change, ensuring your efforts align with the ultimate goal of enhancing work happiness, productivity, stress management, and work-life balance.

First and foremost, understanding the landscape of your organization is vital. This includes recognizing both its strengths and areas ripe for improvement. Change is most effective when it's built on a foundation of recognized need. Identifying specific policies or procedures that are outdated, inefficient, or contributing to workplace stress is your starting point. Gathering qualitative and quantitative data to support your observations is essential, as it lends credibility to your case. This might involve collecting employee feedback, benchmarking against industry standards, or citing research on the impact of certain policies on employee well-being and productivity.

Communication is the heartbeat of change. Developing a clear, concise, and compelling narrative about why change is necessary is one of your most critical tasks. This narrative should not only outline the issues with current policies but also paint a vivid picture of the positive outcomes that could result from change. It's about crafting a story that resonates on a personal level with everyone involved, connecting the dots between improved policies and a more fulfilling work environment.

Empathy plays a significant role in this process. Change often evokes fear and resistance, largely due to the uncertainty it breeds. Acknowledging these feelings and addressing them directly in your case for change is important. Demonstrating how the proposed changes align with the values and goals of the organization and its employees helps in mitigating these concerns. By showing empathy, you're not just advocating for change; you're supporting your colleagues through the transition.

Strategic alliances within the organization can greatly amplify your efforts. Identifying key stakeholders and influencers who share your vision for change can provide a formidable support network. These alliances are crucial for both garnering support and navigating organizational politics. They also serve as a platform for diverse perspectives, making your case for change richer and more inclusive.

Flexibility is another important aspect to consider. Even with a well-crafted case, be prepared to adapt your approach based on feedback and evolving circumstances within the organization. This may mean revising some of your proposals, finding compromises, or even stepping back to reassess the situation. Flexibility does not mean a departure from your core goals but an open-mindedness in how they can be achieved.

An often overlooked but critical component is celebrating small wins. As change is implemented, highlighting early successes can build momentum and demonstrate the tangible benefits of your initiatives. It's an effective way to keep stakeholders engaged and committed to the journey of transformation.

Implementing change also requires patience. The processes and structures within organizations have been built over time and altering them can be a slow endeavor. Patience, persistence, and a focus on long-term goals are essential traits for anyone leading a charge for change.

The power of a well-communicated vision cannot be overstated. People need to see the finish line – what does the future look like with these changes in place? This vision should be inspiring, realistic, and, most importantly, shared. When people feel they are part of something bigger, their investment in the outcome increases.

Feedback mechanisms should be an integral part of your strategy. As changes are proposed and implemented, creating channels for open, honest feedback ensures that the process is inclusive. This not only helps in making adjustments where necessary but also strengthens the sense of community and shared purpose within the organization.

Furthermore, it's crucial to highlight the scalability of proposed changes. Show how these adjustments can grow and evolve with the organization. This forward-thinking approach reassures stakeholders that the proposed changes are not just solutions for today but investments in the future.

Throughout this process, maintaining a balance between assertiveness and receptiveness is key. Being assertive about the need for change while also being open to input and alternate perspectives fosters a collaborative environment. This balance is what ultimately propels a compelling case for change forward.

Building a compelling case for change within the workplace entails a multifaceted approach. It's about seeing the bigger picture, engaging others in your vision, navigating the complexities of organizational dynamics, and, most importantly, driving towards a collective goal of improved workplace well-being and productivity. By following these principles, you are not just advocating for change; you are laying the groundwork for a more vibrant, fulfilling, and balanced work environment.

Remember, change is a marathon, not a sprint. It's about consistent effort, resilient advocacy, and strategic adaptability. With patience and perseverance, the impact of your endeavors can transform your workplace in profound, lasting ways. So take these strategies to heart, and embark on the journey of change with confidence and purpose.

As you move forward, keep revisiting the core motives behind the desire for change. The path to a happier, more productive, and balanced workplace is paved with challenges, but it's also lined with opportunities for growth, learning, and unparalleled satisfaction. Your efforts to build a compelling case for change are not just for the benefit of your own work-life balance but for that of your entire organization.

Navigating Organizational Politics The terrain of any workplace is dotted with the often-invisible landmines of organizational politics. Like a silent current beneath the surface, these dynamics shape decisions, influence careers, and affect the daily lives of everyone from the entry-level employee to the seasoned executive. Understanding how to navigate these waters, therefore, becomes not just a strategy for career advancement but a necessity for maintaining one's well-being and job satisfaction.

In the fabric of workplace relationships, power and influence are currencies. Recognizing who holds these currencies and how they're exchanged is the first step in understanding organizational politics. It's about observing interactions, understanding informal networks, and acknowledging that decision-making often extends beyond official titles and roles. This does not mean one has to manipulate or scheme; rather, it's about being astute, respectful, and ethical in engaging with others.

Building genuine relationships across the organization can serve as both a compass and a shield in navigating workplace politics. By fostering connections based on trust and mutual respect, you develop a network of allies who can offer insights and support when navigating challenging situations. These relationships are built over time, through consistent, positive interactions, and by proving oneself to be reliable, competent, and supportive.

Communication skills are paramount. Articulate your ideas clearly, listen actively, and be open to feedback. However, mastering the art of timing and discretion is equally important. Knowing when to speak up and when to hold back can determine whether your voice adds value or becomes lost in the noise. It's about striking a balance between being assertive and being reflective, ensuring that your contributions are both heard and well-regarded.

The power of observation cannot be overstated. By attentively observing the dynamics around you, you can learn much about the unspoken rules that govern the workplace. Paying attention to how decisions are made, who is involved in those decisions, and how conflicts are resolved can provide valuable insights into the political landscape of your organization.

Manage your visibility strategically. Being visible in the right way—to the right people and at the right times—can have a significant impact on your ability to navigate organizational politics successfully. This means taking on projects or assignments that align with your skills and goals, and that also matter to the organization. It's about contributing in ways that are recognized and valued by those who are in positions to support your career.

Always act with integrity. The realm of workplace politics can sometimes seem murky, but maintaining one's integrity is paramount. This means staying true to your values, delivering on your promises, and being honest in your dealings with others. Even in a competitive environment, long-term respect is garnered through honesty and ethical behavior.

Navigating organizational politics also requires a level of emotional intelligence. Being able to manage your emotions, empathize with others, and handle interpersonal relationships judiciously and empathetically can significantly enhance your political acumen. Understanding your own emotional responses and developing the ability to anticipate and understand the emotions of others can provide a decisive advantage in navigating complex workplace dynamics.

Prepare for setbacks. No journey through the maze of organizational politics is without its setbacks. Missteps can and do happen, and when they do, resilience becomes key. Seeing setbacks not as failures but as learning opportunities can provide the insights needed to navigate more successfully in the future. This resilient mindset, coupled with a commitment to continuous learning, can help you adapt and thrive.

Seek mentors and sponsors. These are individuals who can provide guidance, advocate on your behalf, and open doors to opportunities that might otherwise remain closed. A mentor or sponsor can offer advice rooted in their own experiences, helping you to avoid common pitfalls and to understand the subtleties of your organization's politics. Choosing someone who embodies the qualities you respect and aspire to can make this relationship especially transformative.

Contribute to a positive organizational culture. By embodying and promoting values such as transparency, fairness, and cooperation, you contribute to creating a workplace environment where politics are less about individual agendas and more about collective success. In such an environment, political navigation becomes less about survival and more about contributing to a culture of openness and mutual support.

Nurture your resilience. The ability to bounce back from disappointments and maintain a positive outlook is indispensable in navigating organizational politics. Resilience is not about avoiding challenges but rather about facing them with courage and learning from them. Developing resilience can involve cultivating a network of support, maintaining a healthy work-life balance, and focusing on your well-being.

Navigating organizational politics is an inevitable part of working within any organization. By developing an understanding of these dynamics, building solid relationships, communicating effectively, acting with integrity, and cultivating resilience, you can navigate these waters more successfully. Instead of being swept away by the undercurrents of office politics, you'll find yourself able to chart a course that aligns with your values and professional goals, contributing to not only your success but also the well-being and success of those around you.

The journey through the landscape of organizational politics is ongoing, with each step offering opportunities for growth and understanding. As you continue to navigate these complexities, remember that your actions and decisions not only shape your career but also influence the broader organizational culture. By approaching organizational politics with a mindset of learning, integrity, and positive influence, you can make a meaningful impact, paving the way for a happier, more productive work life.

Chapter 12: Balancing the Scales: Work-Life Integration

In the hustle of meeting deadlines and striving for success, it's easy to let the scales tip heavily towards work, often at the expense of personal life and well-being. Finding equilibrium between these two worlds is not just desirable but essential for long-term happiness and productivity. This chapter aims to unpack the concept of work-life integration, offering practical strategies to navigate this balancing act more gracefully.

Time management sits at the heart of work-life integration. It's about making the most out of the hours we have, ensuring we allocate enough time for work, rest, and play. This involves setting clear boundaries between work and personal time. Establish boundaries that are not just respected by you but also by your colleagues and loved ones, creating a mutual understanding that enhances your ability to juggle various aspects of life.

Cultivating hobbies and interests outside of work plays a crucial role in work-life integration. These activities not only enrich our lives but also boost our mental health and creativity. They offer a counterbalance to workplace stress, providing a necessary diversion and helping to recharge our batteries.

The importance of disconnecting cannot be overstated in today's always-on culture. Regular digital detoxes, where you step away from emails, messages, and work calls, can dramatically improve your mental well-being. It allows you to be present in the moment, enjoying quality time with friends and family without the constant buzz of work in the background.

To begin with, let's delve into strategies for effective time management. Prioritizing tasks, setting realistic goals, and learning to say 'no' are crucial steps in ensuring that work doesn't engulf your entire day. By taking control of your time, you empower yourself to make room for other aspects of life that bring you joy and fulfillment.

Integrating work and personal life also means recognizing when you're stretching yourself too thin. It's about understanding that saying 'yes' to every request or opportunity at work means saying 'no' to something in your personal life. This realignment of priorities requires constant vigilance and the courage to make tough decisions for the sake of your overall well-being.

Learning how to effectively disconnect in our hyper-connected world might seem daunting at first. It begins with small, intentional actions, like turning off notifications after work hours or having phone-free dinners with family. Over time, these actions create a buffer between work and personal life, helping you to decompress and enjoy your downtime fully.

Cultivating hobbies and interests can start small. It could be as simple as dedicating time each week to read, garden, paint, or whatever else brings you a sense of pleasure and accomplishment outside of work. This commitment to personal growth and enjoyment contributes significantly to a more balanced and fulfilling life.

It's also important to foster meaningful connections with family and friends. These relationships are vital for emotional support and happiness. They require time and attention, just like any important project at work. Investing in these personal connections offers a powerful counterweight to the demands of professional life.

In the quest for work-life integration, the role of support systems cannot be underestimated. Whether it's relying on a partner to share household responsibilities or reaching out to colleagues for help in managing workloads, building a network of support promotes a sense of community and shared responsibility. It's a reminder that you're not in this alone and that it's okay to ask for and offer help.

Setting clear expectations at work and home is also key. Transparent communication about your commitments and limitations helps manage the expectations of bosses, coworkers, and family members. It also helps in negotiating workloads and deadlines that respect your personal time and commitments.

Remember, the goal of work-life integration isn't to create a perfect balance, as life's demands are ever-changing. Instead, the aim is to become agile and flexible, adjusting your priorities and commitments as necessary. This adaptability is critical in managing the ebb and flow of work and personal demands with grace and resilience.

Work-life integration is about creating a life that reflects your values, priorities, and personal aspirations. It involves a continuous process of negotiation, compromise, and adjustment to ensure that work enriches rather than depletes your life. By adopting effective time management strategies, cultivating personal interests, and learning to disconnect, you pave the way for a more balanced, fulfilling life.

As we move forward, remember that work-life integration isn't a destination but a journey. It's about making intentional choices every day that align with your vision for a well-rounded and satisfying life. Stepping confidently into this journey requires courage, effort, and the conviction that you deserve to lead a life that is as rich personally as it is professionally.

Ultimately, achieving work-life integration is an investment in your well-being, happiness, and productivity. It's a commitment to living fully, both at work and outside of it, and a testament to the belief that you can create a life that truly reflects your values and ambitions.

Strategies for Time Management As we continue our journey through the labyrinth of workplace well-being, let's delve into the cornerstone of achieving balance: effective time management. Mastering this skill not only bolsters productivity but also serves as an antidote to work-related stress, paving the way for a more fulfilling life both within and beyond the office walls.

Time, unlike any other resource, operates on a fixed continuum; it neither expands nor contracts. Thus, the essence of time management lies not in controlling time itself but in managing how we choose to spend it. This chapter unpacks strategies designed to optimize your daily schedule, ensuring that every tick of the clock moves you closer to your work-life integration goals.

Initiate with a profound understanding of your current time allocation. It's akin to embarking on a journey; knowing your starting point is as crucial as your destination. For a week, meticulously track how you spend your hours, both at work and home. This exercise unveils patterns and habits, some of which may surprise you, highlighting areas where changes could lead to significant improvements in how you manage your time.

Embrace the power of prioritization. Mastering this aspect requires a delicate balance, distinguishing between what is urgent and what is important. Urgent tasks demand immediate attention, but it's the important tasks that contribute to long-term goals and fulfillment. The Eisenhower Matrix, a simple yet effective tool, can assist in categorizing tasks into four quadrants based on urgency and importance, guiding you in focusing on what truly matters.

Establishing boundaries is pivotal. In today's always-on culture, the line between work and personal life blurs easily. Setting clear boundaries with your colleagues, and even with yourself, about when you are available for work-related tasks fosters respect for your time and allows you to recharge. Remember, being constantly available does not equate to being more productive.

Learn to say 'no.' While this may initially feel uncomfortable, especially in a culture that prioritizes hustle over health, declining additional responsibilities that don't align with your priorities or capacity is a vital strategy for time management. It's about making intentional choices, acknowledging that accepting everything often leads to half-hearted efforts and burnout.

Master the art of delegation. Delegating tasks allows you to focus on what you do best while empowering your team. It requires trust and the understanding that perfectionism can be a hindrance to productivity. Giving others the opportunity to contribute and grow not only enhances team dynamics but also frees up your time for tasks that require your unique expertise.

Break down large projects into manageable tasks. Facing a colossal project can feel overwhelming, leading to procrastination. By dissecting it into smaller, more manageable components, you create a series of achievable steps, making it easier to start and maintain momentum. This approach also allows for more accurate time estimation and planning.

Utilize technology wisely. Countless apps and tools promise to revolutionize time management. However, indiscriminate use of technology can become a distraction. Choose tools that seamlessly integrate into your workflow, whether it's a digital planner, task management app, or a simple timer for implementing the Pomodoro Technique, which encourages focused work sessions interspersed with short breaks.

Reflect on and refine your approach. Effective time management isn't a set-it-and-forget-it affair. It demands periodic evaluation and adjustment. What works today may not work tomorrow, as priorities shift and new challenges arise. Regular reflection ensures your strategies remain aligned with your goals, allowing for tweaks and improvements.

Invest in self-care. It may seem counterintuitive to add another activity to your schedule, but allocating time for self-care is an investment with exponential returns. Activities that support physical, emotional, and mental well-being, like exercise, meditation, or simply engaging in a hobby, recharge your batteries, making you more effective in every other aspect of life.

Practice mindfulness. In this high-speed world, our minds often race ahead to the next task before we've completed the current one. Cultivating mindfulness, the art of being fully present in the moment, can enhance productivity and satisfaction. Techniques such as breathing exercises or brief moments of meditation can anchor you in the now, enhancing focus and efficiency.

Plan for interruptions. Despite our best efforts, the workday is rarely interruption-free. Instead of viewing interruptions as setbacks, factor them into your planning. Allotting buffer time between tasks allows for a more flexible approach, adapting to the unpredictable nature of workplace demands without derailing your entire schedule.

Finally, celebrate your successes. Small wins, when acknowledged, build momentum and motivation. Rewarding yourself for managing your time effectively, whether through a small treat or simply taking a moment to reflect on what you've accomplished, can reinforce positive habits and motivate you to continue refining your time management skills.

In mastering time management, we uncover not just the pathway to increased productivity and reduced stress but also the blueprint for a richer, more balanced life. It's about making mindful choices, embracing our limited time, and investing it in the areas of our lives that bring us joy, fulfillment, and growth. By integrating these strategies, we navigate our days with intention, leading to a more rewarding and balanced existence.

Cultivating Hobbies and Interests Outside Work
Stepping outside the boundaries of work commitments and immersing oneself in hobbies and interests seems like a simple piece of advice. However, it's a potent tool for rejuvenating our spirits, creativity, and productivity. In a world where work often consumes a significant part of our waking hours, finding balance through engaging in activities outside of work is not just beneficial; it's essential for sustaining long-term happiness and well-being.

Hobbies provide a unique avenue for stress relief. Engaging in activities that bring joy and satisfaction leads to the production of endorphins, the body's natural stress-relievers. Whether it's painting, gardening, playing a musical instrument, or baking, these activities divert our mind from the pressures of deadlines and expectations, offering a much-needed break.

Moreover, hobbies and interests outside work can significantly enhance our creativity. Often, creative solutions and fresh ideas spring forth not while we are intensely focusing on a problem but when our minds are relaxed and engaged in entirely different activities. The mental break helps us return to work-related challenges with a fresh perspective, often leading to innovative solutions.

Another critical aspect of cultivating hobbies is the development of new skills and knowledge. The learning and growth that occur while pursuing a hobby can be unexpectedly relevant and beneficial to our professional lives. For example, someone who engages in photography might develop an enhanced eye for detail and aesthetics, valuable in roles that require visual presentation skills.

Engaging in activities outside of work also helps in building and strengthening social connections. Joining clubs or groups that share your interests can introduce you to people outside your usual social and professional circles. These interactions can lead to new friendships, providing emotional support and enriching your social life.

Beyond the individual benefits, having hobbies and interests contributes to a more balanced identity. It reminds us that we are not defined solely by our profession or job title. We are complex beings with varied interests and talents, which should be nurtured and celebrated.

In promoting work-life integration, it's crucial to acknowledge the barriers that might prevent someone from pursuing hobbies. Time constraints, high levels of job responsibility, or lack of energy are common challenges. Addressing these requires intentional effort, such as setting aside specific times for leisure activities, and perhaps more importantly, giving oneself permission to take these breaks without feeling guilty.

Moreover, the act of setting boundaries between work and personal life plays a pivotal role. In an era where digital connectivity can blur these lines, it's vital to establish clear boundaries. This might mean turning off work-related notifications after hours or dedicating specific spaces in the home where work cannot intrude, physically or mentally.

Financial constraints can also limit one's ability to engage in certain hobbies. However, it's essential to remember that many rewarding activities require minimal to no expenditure. Exploring nature, engaging in physical exercise, or volunteering are examples of fulfilling hobbies that are not financially burdensome.

The path to integrating hobbies into our lives might also involve rediscovering old passions. Often, the hobbies that brought us immense joy in childhood or early adulthood have been set aside. Revisiting these can reignite a sense of happiness and satisfaction that has been missing.

For individuals struggling to identify hobbies or interests, experimentation is key. Trying out new activities without the pressure of mastery can lead to unexpected discoveries about ourselves and what we enjoy. It's also a reminder that the pursuit of hobbies is not about perfection but about the joy and personal growth that comes from the experience.

Self-reflection plays a critical role in this journey. Understanding what genuinely interests and motivates us outside of work can guide us towards choosing hobbies that fulfill us. This process involves listening to our inner desires and needs, rather than following trends or what others suggest.

Finally, the pursuit of hobbies and interests outside of work should be viewed as an integral component of personal development and well-being, not a luxury or an afterthought. It's an investment in ourselves that pays dividends in all areas of life, including our professional productivity and satisfaction.

Cultivating hobbies and interests outside of work is a multifaceted strategy for enhancing our quality of life. It offers a sanctuary for relaxation, a playground for creativity, a venue for learning, and a foundation for social connection and personal identity. As we navigate the demands of our professional lives, let's not forget the richness and fulfillment that hobbies and interests can bring to our entire being.

The effort to balance work commitments with personal interests and hobbies is not just about managing stress or avoiding burnout; it's about enriching our lives, nurturing our passions, and ultimately, about crafting a more joyful and meaningful existence. As we pursue this balance, we rekindle our enthusiasm for life, both inside and outside the workplace.

The Importance of Disconnecting As we venture deeper into the strategies for achieving a harmonious work-life balance, the concept of disconnecting emerges as a beacon. It's not simply stepping away from work; it's an art—one that nurtures our mental, emotional, and physical well-being. In this era of constant connectivity, the ability to unplug is more than a luxury; it's a crucial ingredient in the recipe for sustaining happiness and productivity at work.

The notion of disconnecting is often misconstrued as abandoning responsibilities or shirking duties. However, it's about creating a deliberate space for ourselves where work does not permeate. This intentional detachment is vital for replenishing our inner reserves. Just as we recharge our smartphones, our minds and bodies need downtime to recharge fully. Without it, we risk burnout—a state all too familiar in today's fast-paced work environments.

Disconnecting allows us to reset our cognitive processes, enabling clearer thinking and problem-solving. When we're constantly bombarded with notifications and demands, our brain's bandwidth is compromised. By stepping away, we clear the mental clutter, giving our brain permission to hit the reset button. This isn't merely theoretical; studies have shown that breaks, even short ones, significantly enhance cognitive performance.

Moreover, the act of disconnecting fosters creativity. Uninterrupted by the constant ping of work-related communications, our minds can wander. It's in these moments of detachment that our brains connect disparate ideas, cultivating the seeds of innovation. Creativity flourishes not in the hustle and bustle, but in quiet and solitude, where thoughts can breathe and ideas can gestate.

On a more personal level, disconnecting strengthens our relationships. In the absence of work distractions, we can fully engage with our loved ones, building deeper connections. These moments nurture our support systems, crucial for navigating stressful periods at work.

Relationships grounded in quality time foster a network of emotional support, offering a buffer against work-related stress.

Disconnecting also invites us to engage in self-reflection. In the silence away from notifications and emails, we can listen to our own thoughts and feelings more clearly. This introspection is valuable for personal growth, helping us identify what truly brings us joy and fulfillment both within and outside our careers. Understanding ourselves better can lead to more informed decisions about our professional paths and personal lives.

Physically, the act of disconnecting helps alleviate the symptoms of chronic stress. Constant engagement with work triggers our body's stress response, a state not meant to be sustained over long periods. By stepping away, we allow our bodies to shift out of this high-alert mode, reducing the risk of stress-related health issues such as hypertension and anxiety disorders.

Practicing disconnection also promotes healthier sleep patterns. The blue light emitted by screens can disrupt our circadian rhythms, making it harder to fall asleep. Reducing screen time, especially before bed, can improve the quality of our sleep, which is essential for cognitive function, mood regulation, and overall health.

It's essential to set boundaries that encourage disconnection. This might mean defining specific work hours, using do-not-disturb functions on our devices, or establishing tech-free zones in our homes. These boundaries aren't just about physical separation from work; they're about creating a psychological barrier that enables us to decompress and rejuvenate.

Employers play a role in supporting disconnection too. Organizations that encourage their employees to take breaks and respect their off-hours contribute to a healthier workplace culture. When companies prioritize the well-being of their staff, they set the stage for increased loyalty, productivity, and satisfaction.

Disconnecting isn't just about taking vacations or long breaks. It's about integrating small moments of disconnection into our daily lives. This could be short walks, mindfulness exercises, or simply sitting quietly without distractions. These brief pauses can dramatically increase our overall sense of well-being and our effectiveness at work.

Yet, disconnecting can be challenging in a culture that glorifies busyness and constant availability. It requires courage to resist the pressure to always be "on." However, the benefits of disconnecting—improved mental health, creativity, relationships, and work satisfaction—are too significant to ignore. It's a courageous act of self-care that says, "I value my well-being."

Finally, it's important to approach disconnecting with compassion and flexibility. There will be times when work demands our attention outside the usual confines. The key is to not let these instances become the norm but rather exceptions. By honoring our need to disconnect regularly, we build resilience, enabling us to handle intense periods of work more effectively.

As we journey towards happier, more productive work lives, let's remember the power of disconnecting. It's about giving ourselves permission to step back, to breathe, and to replenish our spirit. In doing so, we don't just enhance our work performance; we enrich our lives.

The art of disconnecting isn't just a strategy for achieving work-life balance; it's a profound act of self-preservation and self-respect. By embracing periods of disconnection, we open doors to greater creativity, strengthened relationships, and a deeper sense of self-awareness. Let's commit to unplugging, to ensure our work enriches, rather than depletes, our lives.

Chapter 13:
Putting It All Together: A Roadmap to Well-Being

In the previous chapters, we've explored a diverse range of strategies and insights aimed at managing work stress, boosting productivity, and achieving a harmonious work-life balance. Now, it's time to synthesize these elements into a cohesive and personalized roadmap to well-being. As you've journeyed through the pages of this book, you've encountered the mechanics of work stress, the essence of motivation, and the art of navigating interpersonal challenges. Let's now weave these threads into a tapestry that not only illustrates but also guides you towards an enriched professional life.

Creating Your Personal Stress-Management Plan is the cornerstone of our roadmap. Every individual experiences stress differently, which means your plan needs to be custom-tailored to fit your unique needs and circumstances. By combining mindfulness exercises, such as those detailed in Chapter 2, with practical strategies like prioritization and mono-tasking from Chapter 3, you can assemble a robust toolkit. This toolkit should not be static; instead, it should evolve as you gain deeper insights into your stress patterns and coping mechanisms.

Moving forward, **Implementing a Sustainable Routine** becomes paramount. Sustainability in routines is not just about consistency; it's about flexibility and adaptability. Incorporate regular breaks, exercise, and hobbies as non-negotiable elements of your daily schedule, akin to the advice offered in Chapter 6 and Chapter 12. Remember, achieving work-life balance doesn't mean dividing your time equally but rather allocating it in a way that nourishes both your professional and personal growth.

The journey to well-being is, inherently, ongoing. Thus, **Continual Self-Assessment and Adjustment** is critical. Just as businesses conduct quarterly reviews to gauge progress, set new goals, and adjust strategies, you should periodically reassess your well-being plan. Are the strategies you're employing effective? Do your goals still align with your values and aspirations? This cyclic process ensures that your roadmap remains relevant and responsive to your evolving life context.

Interestingly, well-being is not just a personal affair; it has ripples that can influence your surroundings. As you implement your personalized roadmap, you'll likely become a beacon of positivity and resilience in your workplace. This isn't a byproduct—it's a testament to the transformative power of taking charge of your well-being. You'll find that, by fostering a healthier work-life, you might inspire others to embark on similar journeys of self-discovery and improvement.

The idea of creating and maintaining a personalized roadmap might seem daunting at first. It requires honesty, commitment, and, above all, a willingness to venture into uncharted territories within yourself. But take heart in knowing that each step taken is a step closer to mastering the equilibrium between your professional endeavors and personal well-being. This equilibrium is not fixed; it sways and adjusts, much like a dancer responding intuitively to the rhythm of life.

Through the continuous process of self-assessment and adjustment, you'll cultivate a keen sense of awareness about what truly matters. This awareness allows you to navigate stress, not by avoiding it altogether but by understanding its contours and learning how to move through it with grace and resilience. Stress, after all, is not the enemy—it's a signal, a prompt to engage more deeply with ourselves and our environment.

And so, as we draw near the close of this chapter, it's essential to recognize that well-being is not a destination but a journey. It's a journey marked not by milestones of achievements but by the quality of your experiences and relationships. The roadmap you create isn't just a plan; it's a reflection of your commitment to living a balanced, fulfilling life.

Implementing the strategies discussed in this book requires time and patience. Success won't come overnight, nor will it always be smooth. There will be days of setback, and that's okay. What's important is the resilience to stand back up, the flexibility to adjust your plan, and the courage to continue moving forward.

In the end, your roadmap to well-being is a living document, a narrative that's continuously written and rewritten. It's a guide that not only navigates you through the complexities of the work environment but also enriches your life with deeper meaning and purpose. As you turn the pages of this chapter to the next, carry forward the knowledge, strategies, and insights, but most importantly, carry forward a steadfast commitment to your well-being. For in doing so, you'll not only transform your work and personal life but also become a catalyst for positive change in the lives of those around you.

Creating Your Personal Stress-Management Plan
As we nestle into this critical chapter, we're at the nexus of transforming understanding into action. You've navigated the complexities of work stress, discovered the multiplicity of strategies to handle overwhelming feelings and distractions, and explored avenues for securing your worth and advocating for workplace accommodations.

Now, it's time to tailor these insights into a coherent, personalized stress-management plan that not only mitigates stress but also fortifies your well-being, autonomy, and satisfaction at work.

To start with, let's establish a foundational belief: managing stress isn't about eradicating it completely, but rather adapting to its presence productively. Stress, when managed effectively, can serve as a motivator, a catalyst for growth and learning. The first step in devising your plan is to conduct a self-assessment. Recognize the stress triggers identified in previous discussions, scrutinize your responses to these triggers, and assess the efficiency of your coping mechanisms. This introspection is vital in laying down the skeleton of your personalized plan.

Following this, clarity on your boundaries is paramount. Setting boundaries is an art; it's about understanding where you draw your lines with tasks, interactions, and even your own ambitions. Ask yourself, "What aspects of my work and interactions drain my energy, and how can I protect myself?" Setting these boundaries will help preserve your energy and focus on what truly matters.

Next, intertwine the practice of mindfulness and positive self-talk into your daily routine. Mindfulness, a state of active, open attention to the present, can transform stress into a moment of engagement and observation, rather than a trigger for anxiety. Positive self-talk, on the other hand, rebuilds the narrative you tell yourself about your capabilities and worth, fortifying you against the effects of stress.

Another essential pillar is the adoption of an active lifestyle outside work. Exercise, as discussed, is a potent stress-reliever. It's also a testament to the power of taking regular breaks to rejuvenate your mind and body, sustaining your energy levels, and improving cognitive functions and emotional resilience.

As you build your plan, remember the importance of regular breaks. Integrate short, consistent breaks into your workday to recalibrate and prevent burnout. These pauses are not merely escapes but opportunities to refresh and gain new perspectives on challenging tasks.

Pivotal to your stress-management plan is the cultivation of hobbies and interests outside of work. Engaging in activities that you are passionate about can serve as an effective counterbalance to work stress, enriching your personal identity beyond your professional role.

On the interpersonal front, forge positive relationships at work. Seek out peers or mentors who can offer support, guidance, and a sounding board for your ideas and frustrations. These connections can significantly bolster your emotional resilience and provide a sense of belonging and community.

Embrace the art of prioritization. Not every email demands an instant reply, and not every task needs to be completed by the end of the day. Distinguish between what's urgent and what can wait. This will help you manage your energy and focus on tasks that are truly consequential.

Leverage technology to streamline your tasks but do so judiciously. Technology can be a double-edged sword; it can enhance efficiency but also fuel distractions. Use apps and tools that aid in minimizing distractions and organizing your tasks more effectively.

Don't overlook the magic of mono-tasking. While multitasking might seem like a productivity hack, it often leads to divided attention and increased stress. Commit to one task at a time, and immerse yourself fully for more efficient and high-quality output.

At the heart of your plan should be setting and achieving small wins. These milestones, no matter how minor, are crucial for motivation maintenance. They provide a sense of progress and accomplishment, fueling your drive to tackle larger challenges.

Finding your 'why' is also essential. Connect your work to your personal goals and values. Understanding the impact of your work and how it aligns with your broader life objectives can infuse your daily tasks with meaning and motivation.

In constructing your personal stress-management plan, flexibility is key. Allow your plan to be a living document that evolves as you gain deeper insights into your stress triggers, coping mechanisms, and what strategies are most effective for you. Experiment, adjust, and refine your plan based on your changing needs and circumstances.

Finally, don't go at it alone. Engage in continual dialogues with mentors, peers, and professionals who can provide external perspectives, support, and guidance. Your journey towards managing stress and fostering well-being at work is a collective endeavor, enriched by the wisdom and experiences of those around you.

With these components in place, you're well on your way to developing a comprehensive, personalized stress-management plan. This plan is not just about surviving the workday; it's about thriving, finding joy and fulfillment in your work, and maintaining a harmonious balance between your professional and personal life.

Implementing a Sustainable Routine As we dive into the heart of establishing routines that echo the harmony of productivity and well-being, it's essential to remember the why behind our actions. A sustainable routine isn't just about checking off tasks; it's about creating a rhythm that supports our mental, emotional, and physical health. This path to a balanced life, where work and joy coexist, requires thoughtful planning and a steadfast commitment to self-care.

Our journey begins with the acknowledgment of our personal peaks and valleys throughout the day. Understanding when you're most alert and creative, versus when you need rest, can shape a routine that feels almost effortlessly productive. It's about syncing with your natural rhythms, not fighting against them. This alignment empowers us to tackle demanding tasks when we're at our peak and allows for gentler activities during our downtimes, ensuring a steady flow of accomplishment without the burnout.

Prioritization is the anchor of any effective routine. By defining what truly matters, both on a daily and long-term basis, we can avoid the trap of busywork and focus our energies on impactful actions. This not just boosts our productivity but also nurtures a sense of achievement and satisfaction. It's crucial, then, to regularly assess and adjust our priorities to reflect our current objectives and values.

Beyond the to-do lists, fostering time for creativity and pauses is vital. Creativity doesn't thrive on constant go-mode; it requires space to breathe and meander, allowing fresh ideas and solutions to surface. Similarly, pauses or breaks are not signs of weakness but rather strategic decisions to refuel and gain clarity. They are the unsung heroes of sustained productivity and innovation.

Embracing the art of delegation and saying no is a skill that bolsters the durability of our routine. By realistically assessing our bandwidth and leveraging the strengths of others, we can lighten our load and concentrate on areas where we can make the most significant difference. Learning to say 'no', or 'not now', protects our energy and respects the limits of our capacity, ensuring we remain effective and engaged.

Creating a distraction-free environment is another cornerstone of a sustainable routine. In a world teeming with digital interruptions and the constant buzz of connectivity, carving out a quiet space where focus can flourish is essential. This might mean setting boundaries around technology use, designing a physical workspace that minimizes distractions, or identifying times of day that are reserved for deep work.

Physical wellness is certainly linked to our ability to maintain a productive routine. Regular exercise, nutritious food, and adequate sleep form the triad of basic needs that fuel our bodies and minds. When these needs are met, we're better equipped to handle stress, make decisions, and stay motivated. Ignoring these aspects can derail even the most well-intentioned plans.

Mental and emotional wellness, too, demands our attention. Implementing practices like mindfulness, gratitude, or journaling into our routine can provide us with tools to navigate the inevitable highs and lows with greater resilience. These practices help to cultivate a mindset focused on growth and learning, transforming challenges into opportunities for development.

Establishing a support network—whether it's colleagues, mentors, friends, or family—can significantly enhance the sustainability of our routines. They offer us a sounding board for ideas, a source of encouragement during tough times, and can provide accountability and perspective that enrich our journey. Sharing our goals and struggles opens the door for collaboration and mutual support, amplifying our efforts and outcomes.

Flexibility, perhaps paradoxically, is a critical component of a sustainable routine. While consistency helps to build habits, rigidity can lead to frustration and stagnation. Life is unpredictable, and our routines need to adapt to shifting circumstances. Embracing change with a problem-solving mindset allows us to navigate disruptions with grace, finding new paths to our goals.

Regular reflection and self-assessment are key practices in maintaining a routine that serves us. By periodically reviewing what's working and what's not, we can make informed adjustments, ensuring our routine evolves in alignment with our changing needs and goals. This reflective practice keeps us connected to our purpose and helps to prevent drift.

Integrating our work and personal lives in a way that feels balanced and fulfilling is an ongoing process. Rather than enforcing strict boundaries, finding ways to blend the two seamlessly—acknowledging that each influences and enriches the other—can lead to a more holistic sense of satisfaction and accomplishment. It's about creating harmony, not compartmentalizing our lives.

Moreover, cultivating hobbies and interests outside of work can significantly contribute to a sustainable routine. They provide an outlet for stress, stimulate creativity, and invite joy and relaxation into our lives. These activities remind us that we are more than our work and that taking time to pursue passions can make us better at our jobs.

Finally, the adoption of a sustainable routine is a deeply personal journey. It's not about replicating someone else's formula for success but discovering what works uniquely for you. It requires patience, experimentation, and self-compassion, recognizing that setbacks are part of the process. By committing to this path, we open ourselves to a life of greater balance, fulfillment, and well-being, both at work and beyond.

Implementing a sustainable routine is the pillar upon which our well-being rests in the modern workspace. It's about more than just productivity; it's about creating a life that feels good to live, where work is a part of our happiness, not a hindrance to it. With intentional action, reflection, and a commitment to self-care, we can craft routines that sustain us through the challenges and rewards of our careers. Let's embrace this journey with open hearts and minds, ready to discover the balance that works best for us.

Continual Self-Assessment and Adjustment As we navigate through the complex landscape of our professional lives, it's essential that we pause regularly to reflect on our journey. This self-reflection isn't merely about celebrating our victories or sulking over our defeats. Rather, it's a strategic pit stop in our marathon, where we assess our running form, our pace, and whether we're still on the right path.

Imagine, for a moment, that you're a gardener. Your career and well-being are the garden you're tending to. Just as a gardener must continually assess the health of their plants, adjusting water and sunlight as needed, you too must continually assess and adjust your strategies for managing work stress and maintaining work-life balance. This process of self-assessment and adjustment is fluid, requiring attentiveness to the ever-changing conditions of your environment.

Why is self-assessment so critical? At its core, it enables you to recognize when something isn't working. Whether it's a particular technique to manage distractions or a method for prioritizing tasks, what works today might not work tomorrow. The world of work is dynamic, with shifting priorities, new challenges, and evolving personal goals. As such, our approaches must be equally dynamic, adapting to the internal and external changes that influence our work and life.

A key part of self-assessment is setting aside time for this practice. It can't be an afterthought or something done only when things go awry. Regularly scheduled check-ins, be they daily, weekly, or monthly, allow you the space to evaluate your current state without the cloud of immediate stress or pressure. During these moments, ask yourself: Are my current strategies effective? Do I find joy and satisfaction in my work? How am I managing stress?

Another dimension of self-assessment involves soliciting feedback from others. Often, we are our own harshest critics, or conversely, we might overlook areas needing improvement. Trusted colleagues, mentors, or even friends can provide external perspectives, helping to illuminate areas of our work life that we might be too close to see clearly.

Adjustment, the natural partner of assessment, involves taking the insights gleaned from your reflections and feedback and translating them into action. This could mean tweaking your daily routine, seeking new strategies for motivation, or even more significant changes, like pursuing new professional opportunities.

It's important to approach adjustment with a mindset of experimentation. Not every change will yield positive outcomes, and that's okay. Each attempt is a learning opportunity, guiding you closer to finding what works best for you in achieving a satisfying and productive work life.

Perpetual learning is a cornerstone of self-assessment and adjustment. As you experiment with different strategies to enhance your work-life balance and productivity, you're gaining valuable insights into what fuels your motivation and what drains it. This knowledge is power, equipping you to make more informed decisions about your professional journey.

The process of self-assessment and adjustment also requires patience and compassion towards oneself. Change doesn't happen overnight, and setbacks are an inevitable part of the journey. Treating yourself with the same understanding and kindness you would offer a friend is essential in navigating this process.

Moreover, celebrating small victories plays a crucial role in maintaining motivation through this continual cycle of assessment and adjustment. Acknowledge and take pride in the steps you've taken, no matter how small they may seem. These mini-celebrations serve as reminders of your progress and the efficacy of your self-reflection process.

In the grand tapestry of your career, it's also vital to recognize that some factors are beyond your control. External changes within your organization or industry may necessitate shifts in your approach. In these instances, the ability to adapt – a skill honed through regular self-assessment and adjustment – becomes invaluable. It enables you to remain resilient in the face of change, finding new ways to achieve balance and fulfillment.

As you implement adjustments, document your journey. Keeping a journal or log of the changes you've made, how they've impacted you, and what outcomes have ensued can be incredibly insightful. This record not only serves as a personal artifact of your growth but also as a practical tool for future self-assessment cycles. It helps you identify patterns, understand what's worked (and what hasn't), and reminds you of how far you've come.

Finally, be open to revisiting and revising your goals. What constitutes a satisfying work-life balance or a productive workday may evolve as you progress through different stages of your career and life. This openness to reevaluation ensures that your efforts in self-assessment and adjustment are always aligned with your current aspirations and needs.

The journey to well-being and satisfaction at work is ongoing, woven from a tapestry of experiences, insights, and adjustments. Embracing the process of continual self-assessment and adjustment equips you with the agility, resilience, and self-awareness needed to navigate the unpredictable waters of professional life. It's about being proactive, not reactive, and always moving towards greater harmony between your work and personal life. Through this attentive and intentional approach, you can cultivate a work-life landscape that is not only productive but deeply fulfilling.

Remember, the goal is not to reach a static state of 'perfect balance' but to engage in a dynamic process of growth and adaptation. The garden of your career and well-being requires ongoing care, and you are the gardener, equipped with the tools of self-assessment and adjustment. Embrace this role with curiosity and compassion, and watch as your garden flourishes.

Chapter 14:
Staying Agile: Adapting to Changing Work Environments

In an era where change is the only constant, an ability to adapt to different work environments with agility is invaluable. We've traversed topics from managing work stress to creating a sustainable routine for well-being. Now, it's crucial to focus on how we can remain flexible and embrace the ebbs and flows that come with evolving workspaces. Change often carries a negative connotation, causing anxiety and resistance. However, viewing change as an opportunity rather than a setback can transform the way we approach our careers. Embracing change positively allows us to lead with curiosity, opening doors to new challenges and growth opportunities.

Learning new skills for career resilience is akin to adding arrows to your quiver. The landscape of work is morphing rapidly, with advancements in technology and shifts in societal needs. Stagnation is the antithesis of growth. Thus, the pursuit of continuous learning not only enhances our skill set but also fortifies our value in the marketplace. It's about being proactive rather than reactive, foreseeing potential shifts in our industry, and equipping ourselves with the knowledge and skills to navigate these changes. This mindset of perpetual learning cultivates a sense of preparedness, no matter the direction in which the tides of change may flow.

Keeping a future-focused mindset is essential. It involves not just surviving but thriving in changing work environments. This orientation enables us to envision a future where we are not just participants but pioneers of change. It's about setting goals that are aligned not only with our personal aspirations but also with foreseeable future trends. Keeping an eye on the horizon helps us to anticipate and prepare for what's coming next, thereby transforming potential challenges into stepping stones for success. In doing so, we maintain our relevance and continue to contribute meaningfully to our workplaces, irrespective of the inevitable shifts that lie ahead.

Embracing Change Positively Change is often the only constant in our work life. Our journey through these chapters has prepared us for many aspects of workplace challenges and personal growth. However, one of the most pivotal skills that remain is the art of embracing change with a positive mindset. Change can be unsettling, it can disrupt our rhythm, challenge our competencies, and even threaten our sense of security. Yet, it is also a powerful catalyst for growth, innovation, and discovering new horizons of personal and professional fulfillment.

Understanding that change is inevitable helps us to shift our perspective from seeing it as an insurmountable obstacle to viewing it as an opportunity. This mindset transformation is fundamental. It's not just about coping with change but thriving in it, leveraging the flux to propel ourselves forward. The first step is to foster a positive outlook towards change. By doing so, we buffer ourselves against the initial shock and discomfort that change can bring.

To truly embrace change positively, it's crucial to cultivate adaptability. Being adaptable doesn't mean losing your sense of self or your core values; instead, it's about being flexible in your methods and open to new experiences. Adaptability is the bridge that allows us to navigate from familiar shores to uncharted territories with confidence and grace.

Another key component is resilience. Change can sometimes lead to setbacks or failures. Building resilience empowers us to bounce back from these situations, learn from them, and continue moving forward. This resilience is cultivated not through avoiding challenges but by facing them head-on, learning from each experience, and growing our emotional and mental fortitude.

Communicating effectively is also paramount in times of change. Whether it's seeking clarification, expressing concerns, or offering suggestions, open communication helps mitigate misunderstandings and builds a supportive network. Sharing our experiences and feelings with colleagues can create a sense of solidarity, making the journey through change less isolating.

Staying informed is equally important. Change often comes with new tools, processes, or expectations. By proactively seeking out information and training, we equip ourselves with the knowledge needed to navigate these new waters. Learning becomes a continuous process, and embracing change means being a perpetual student, eager to grow and evolve.

Setting realistic expectations for oneself during times of change can alleviate much of the stress involved. It's understandable to not have all the answers right away or to feel proficient in new areas immediately. Granting ourselves the patience to learn and adapt at a comfortable pace removes unnecessary pressure and fosters a healthier transition.

Finding meaning in change can transform the way we perceive and interact with it. When we connect changes in our work life to our personal goals and values, the motivation to engage with these changes becomes intrinsic. This alignment of personal and professional growth is what turns change from a hurdle to an engaging challenge worth pursuing.

Seeking and offering support is a cornerstone in positively dealing with change. Whether it's through mentorship, collaboration, or shared learning opportunities, supporting each other fosters a culture of empathy and understanding that makes any transition smoother and more rewarding.

Maintaining a balance between work and personal life is crucial, especially during times of change. It's easy to become consumed by the demands of adapting to new situations. Ensuring that we carve out time for relaxation, hobbies, and personal connections keeps us grounded and prevents burnout.

Facing change with a sense of curiosity rather than fear opens up a world of possibilities. When we approach new situations with a desire to learn and explore, we naturally find ourselves more open to the opportunities change presents. This curiosity can lead to innovations, personal breakthroughs, and discovering new passions.

Remembering to celebrate progress, no matter how small, reinforces a positive attitude toward change. Recognizing and appreciating the steps we've taken in adapting to new situations bolsters our confidence and motivates us to continue moving forward.

Finally, embracing change is about letting go of the need for control. While it's important to steer our course with intention, understanding that many aspects of change are beyond our direct influence helps relieve the tension associated with transitions. Trusting in our ability to adapt and find solutions frees us from the paralysis of perfectionism and fear.

As we continue on our paths, the lessons learned in the face of change will be some of the most valuable. They teach us about our resilience, our adaptability, and our capacity for growth. Change, therefore, is not just a challenge to overcome but an invitation to evolve.

Embracing change positively is a multifaceted endeavor that requires adaptability, resilience, effective communication, and continuous learning. It's about finding balance, seeking and offering support, and maintaining a curious and open mindset. Change is an inevitable part of our professional journey, but with the right attitude and strategies, it can be a powerful force for personal and professional development.

Learning New Skills for Career Resilience In a rapidly evolving job market, staying agile and adaptable isn't just recommended; it's essential for survival and growth. The act of learning new skills serves as your bridge over the waters of uncertainty, ensuring you remain not just relevant, but ahead of the curve. This journey of continuous improvement doesn't merely add lines to your resume; it deepens your understanding of your abilities, the world around you, and how you can contribute to it more meaningfully.

Consider the wave of technological advancements that redefine job roles every few years. It's not the strongest who survive this relentless tide, nor the most intelligent, but those most adaptable to change. Learning new skills—the right ones—becomes our lifeboat, crafted not from wood and nails, but from curiosity, effort, and the willingness to step out of our comfort zones.

To embark on this journey effectively, start with a self-assessment. Reflect on your current skill set and review it against the backdrop of your industry's future demands. This isn't about predicting the future with absolute certainty—none can—but about tuning into trends and signals that suggest where your field is heading. It's about asking yourself, "What can I learn today that will help me tomorrow?"

Once you've identified potential skills to acquire, the question becomes how to learn them. Herein lies a beautiful truth about our modern world: never before have so many resources been so accessible to so many. Online courses, workshops, webinars, podcasts, and even virtual reality simulations offer a plethora of ways to gain new knowledge. And often, the first step is as simple as making a commitment and clicking 'enroll'.

Yet, embarking on this learning journey demands more than just signing up; it requires persistence. The excitement of the initial sign-up fades quickly when faced with the day-to-day reality of fitting this new learning into our already busy lives. This is where the real resilience is built—not in the completion of the course, but in the daily commitment to growth despite the myriad of easier choices available to us.

Learning new skills is also deeply personal. What drives one person may not drive another. It's about finding your motivation, your 'why'. Connecting the skill you're learning to a personal goal or dream can transform the experience from a mere task on your to-do list to a stepping stone towards a vision you have for your life. This sense of purpose fuels persistence, making the learning journey more engaging and fulfilling.

Furthermore, learning is not an isolated activity; it's a communal one. Engaging with a community of learners can significantly enhance your experience. Whether it's through online forums, study groups, or attending conferences, being part of a community provides support, deepens learning through discussion, and often, opens doors to opportunities that wouldn't have existed in isolation.

One must also embrace the mindset of being a forever student. The landscape of most industries today is one of constant change. What is cutting-edge now may be obsolete tomorrow. Accepting that learning is a lifelong endeavor can transform how we approach our careers. It's not a series of sprints to each new skill or job title, but a marathon—a continuous journey of growth and adaptation.

Imagination plays a crucial role in this process as well. Visualizing not just the end goal but the steps to get there can be a powerful motivator. It's about seeing the potential future self you're building with each new skill and understanding the impact you could make in your field, community, or even on a global scale.

Yet, it's also necessary to balance ambition with self-compassion. The road to acquiring new skills is strewn with challenges and failures. Approaching these obstacles with kindness towards oneself, viewing them as learning opportunities rather than roadblocks, can make the journey more sustainable and enjoyable.

Moreover, it's important to celebrate small victories along the way. Setting and achieving micro-goals not only maintains motivation but also builds confidence. Acknowledging the progress made, no matter how minor it seems, reinforces the belief in one's ability to learn and grow.

Integrating these new skills into your current role where possible can also be beneficial. It allows you to test and refine your learning in real-world scenarios, demonstrating your initiative and value to your employer, and potentially opening up new opportunities within your existing career path.

Yet, it's crucial to remain patient and realistic. Skill acquisition takes time, and true mastery even longer. Setting expectations too high, too soon can lead to frustration and burnout. It's a journey of thousands of steps, and it's okay to move at a pace that's sustainable for you.

Learning new skills for career resilience is a multifaceted process that spans knowing what to learn, how to learn, and how to integrate learning into one's life and work. It's a journey that requires curiosity, commitment, community, and compassion—towards oneself and others. By embracing this journey, we not only secure our place in the future of work but also embark on a path of personal fulfillment and contribution to the world around us.

As we look to the horizon, let's move forward with an open heart and a keen mind, ready to embrace the lessons and opportunities that await. For in learning, we not only adapt; we thrive.

Keeping a Future-Focused Mindset As we delve deeper into the nuances of adapting to changing work environments, one foundational pillar cannot be overlooked: the cultivation of a future-focused mindset.

This mindset is pivotal not only to career resilience but also to achieving overarching satisfaction and well-being in one's professional journey. It's about being purposefully present while setting the stage for future success, a delicate balance between navigating present demands and anticipating tomorrow's challenges.

At its core, a future-focused mindset involves envisioning where you want to be and understanding that the decisions you make today are stepping stones towards that destination. It's a stance of strategic foresight, coupled with the realization that the future is not merely a place you arrive at but one you actively create through present actions and attitudes.

In the realm of work, such a mindset encourages a proactive approach to career development and stress management. Stress, after all, often stems from uncertainties or concerns about the future. By adopting a forward-thinking approach, you can mitigate these stresses by feeling more in control and prepared for what lies ahead. This doesn't mean having all the answers now but cultivating confidence in your ability to navigate and adapt as necessary.

Future-focused thinking also fosters continuous learning. The landscape of work is ever-evolving, with new technologies, methodologies, and industry benchmarks emerging. By nurturing a mindset that is always looking ahead, you'll be more inclined to invest in personal and professional development opportunities that enhance your adaptability and relevance in your field. This learning orientation makes you not just a passenger but a pilot of your career trajectory.

An essential element of keeping a future-focused mindset is goal setting. Setting clear, achievable goals provides a roadmap and a measure of progress. It instils a sense of purpose and direction, which is incredibly motivating during times of uncertainty or when faced with daunting challenges. Goals tether your current efforts to future outcomes, making the daily grind more meaningful and fulfilling.

However, it's crucial to maintain flexibility in your goals and plans. The future is inherently unpredictable, and rigidity can lead to frustration. Embrace a mindset that is open to adjustments and pivots, viewing them not as setbacks but as necessary evolutions towards your ultimate objectives. This adaptability is a cornerstone of resilience, ensuring you can weather changes without losing sight of your north star.

Embedded in the future-focused mindset is an optimistic outlook. Optimism doesn't mean ignoring challenges or potential pitfalls but rather approaching them with the belief that they can be overcome or turned into opportunities. Such positivity fuels persistence and creativity, both of which are vital for long-term success and satisfaction in one's career.

Fostering a future-focused mindset also means prioritizing self-care and well-being. After all, the future you aspire to can only be realized if you are physically, mentally, and emotionally equipped to pursue and achieve it. This involves recognizing and managing stress, ensuring adequate rest and recreation, and nurturing relationships that support and inspire you.

Practicing gratitude is another component of a future-focused mindset. While setting sights on future achievements, don't overlook the value of present experiences and accomplishments. Gratitude grounds you in the present, enriching your professional journey and buffering against burnout. It helps you maintain perspective, reminding you of progress made and lessons learned, which inform and facilitate future endeavors.

Another strategy is embracing mentorship, both as a mentor and a mentee. Mentorship offers perspective, advice, and insights that can shape your approach to future challenges and opportunities. It's a symbiotic relationship where shared experiences and wisdom not only guide your path but also enrich the professional growth of those you mentor.

Visualization is a powerful tool in the arsenal of someone with a future-focused mindset. Regularly visualizing your goals and aspirations can make them more concrete and attainable, reinforcing your commitment and actions towards achieving them. This practice also enhances motivation, especially when faced with obstacles, by keeping the rewards of your efforts vividly in your mind's eye.

Networking shouldn't be underestimated either. Building and nurturing a network of professional contacts is akin to laying the groundwork for future opportunities. These connections can open doors to new possibilities, offer support and advice, and provide encouragement. A robust network ensures you're not navigating your career trajectory in isolation but are buoyed by a community of like-minded individuals committed to mutual success.

To truly embed a future-focused mindset into your professional life, it's imperative to periodically review and assess your goals, strategies, and progress. This ongoing evaluation ensures your actions remain aligned with your aspirations and allows you to course-correct as needed. It's a practice that emphasizes intentionality in your career progression, making your future achievements not a matter of chance but a result of deliberate planning and effort.

Cultivating a future-focused mindset is more than a strategic advantage in navigating work environments—it's a comprehensive approach to professional and personal fulfillment. By envisioning the future, setting goals, embracing learning, and maintaining flexibility and optimism, you lay the foundation for a resilient, rewarding career marked by continuous growth and achievement. Remember, the future is not just something you anticipate; it's something you actively shape with each decision and action you take today.

As we move forward, it becomes evident that nurturing a future-focused mindset is not just an individual endeavor but a collective one. Encouraging and supporting each other in our aspirations can amplify our potential for success and satisfaction, highlighting the interconnectedness of our professional journeys. Let's stride into the future with intention, resilience, and optimism, ever mindful of the power we hold to craft the destinies we desire.

Chapter 15: Cultivating a Positive Workplace Culture

Continuing from our exploration of adapting to changing environments, let's shift our focus towards cultivating a workplace culture that not only embraces change but thrives in it. A positive workplace culture fosters a supportive, energetic, and productive environment. It rests on pillars such as transparency, respect, and collective growth. Every individual, from the leadership to new hires, plays a crucial role in fostering this environment.

Leading by example is the cornerstone of cultivating a positive culture. It's about actions speaking louder than words. When leaders demonstrate qualities such as empathy, resilience, and openness to feedback, they set a tone that encourages others to mirror these behaviors. It's akin to setting the rhythm in a piece of music, where each note played by the leader is harmoniously followed by the rest of the team, creating a symphony of productivity and positivity.

However, a vibrant culture isn't just the responsibility of those at the top. Encouraging team wellness is a collective effort that requires input and commitment from everyone. Activities that promote physical health, mental well-being, and emotional balance should be integrated into the workplace. Simple initiatives like mindfulness sessions, having a 'quiet zone' for recharge, or regular health and wellness workshops can have profound effects on the team's overall morale and productivity.

Building a supportive community is another critical aspect. It's about creating a network within the workplace where successes are celebrated, challenges are addressed collectively, and failures are viewed as opportunities for learning and growth. Such a community encourages taking risks and innovation, as there's a safety net of support and understanding.

In nurturing this supportive community, communication plays a pivotal role. Open, honest, and compassionate dialogue helps in resolving conflicts efficiently, boosts collaboration, and enhances the quality of relationships at work. It's like the glue that holds the pieces together, ensuring that the fabric of the workplace culture remains strong and cohesive.

Respect for diversity and inclusivity also contributes significantly to a positive workplace culture. When team members feel valued and included, regardless of their background, skills, or beliefs, it elevates the collective intelligence of the team and sparks creativity. This diversity of thought and perspective is a rich soil from which innovative ideas can grow.

Feedback loops are vital for sustaining a vibrant culture. Regularly soliciting and acting on feedback demonstrates a commitment to continuous improvement and personal development. It reassures the team that their voice is not only heard but valued and considered in shaping the workplace environment.

Recognition and appreciation play a transformative role in building a positive workplace. Small acts of acknowledgment, whether it's a shoutout during a team meeting or a personal note of thanks, can light up an individual's day and reinforce their sense of purpose and value in the team.

Fostering a positive workplace culture is an ongoing journey, not a destination. It requires patience, consistency, and genuine effort from everyone involved. As the culture evolves, it's important to celebrate the milestones achieved and reflect on the lessons learned, using them as a foundation for future growth.

Cultivating a positive workplace culture is a multifaceted process that encompasses leading by example, nurturing wellness, building a supportive community, and embracing diversity and feedback. When we commit to these principles, we pave the way for a workplace that's not only productive but also joyous, resilient, and profoundly satisfying.

Leading by Example When we talk about fostering a positive workplace culture, the cornerstone of such an environment invariably comes down to the leaders and how they conduct themselves. It's a domino effect; the behavior of those at the top trickles down to every level of the organization. Arguably, nothing is more infectious within a workplace than the attitude and actions of its leaders. Leading by example isn't just a catchphrase; it's a powerful strategy for motivating and engaging employees, reducing stress, and enhancing overall productivity.

Imagine walking into an office where the leaders are approachable, practice what they preach, and are the first to roll up their sleeves when the going gets tough. This kind of leadership doesn't just inspire respect; it deepens trust and loyalty, creating a ripple effect throughout the entire organization. It encourages a culture where people feel valued, understood, and, most importantly, part of a team striving towards a common goal.

Leading by example means embodying the work ethics you want to see in your team. It involves setting a benchmark for quality, punctuality, and professionalism. When leaders demonstrate commitment to their tasks, they silently communicate those expectations to their team. This isn't about setting unrealistic standards or expecting people to stretch themselves thin; it's about showing that with dedication and focus, challenges can be overcome, and goals can be achieved.

Moreover, leaders who lead by example are mindful of their work-life balance. They understand the importance of taking breaks, prioritizing mental health, and cultivating interests outside work. By doing so, they not only enrich their own lives but also signal to their employees that taking care of oneself isn't just permitted; it's encouraged. This approach can significantly reduce work stress, as it underlines the organization's commitment to the well-being of its members.

Effective communication is another aspect where leading by example plays a crucial role. Leaders who are clear, transparent, and compassionate in their communication set a standard for the rest of the team. This fosters an environment where everyone feels comfortable voicing their thoughts, concerns, and ideas, knowing they will be received respectfully. In such an atmosphere, stress related to misunderstandings or feeling unheard drastically diminishes.

Moreover, leading by example involves recognizing and acknowledging the hard work and achievements of team members. Leaders who celebrate successes, provide constructive feedback, and support their team in times of failure create a positive and motivating work environment. This not only reduces stress but also boosts morale and productivity.

However, leading by example is not without its challenges. It requires leaders to be consistently self-aware, reflective, and willing to admit their mistakes. Authentic leadership means showing vulnerability at times, acknowledging when you're wrong, and taking steps to correct your course. This openness humanizes leaders, making them more relatable and trustworthy to their team.

Leaders who advocate for and personally engage in professional development set a powerful example as well. They show that learning is a lifelong process, encouraging their team to pursue their own growth opportunities. This attitude towards continuous improvement can alleviate stress by framing challenges as opportunities to learn and evolve rather than insurmountable obstacles.

Additionally, leading by example in today's ever-changing work environment means embracing flexibility and adaptability. Leaders who show that they're open to new ideas, willing to pivot when necessary, and capable of navigating uncertainties demonstrate resilience. This not only reduces stress but also prepares the team to handle change with a more positive mindset.

Furthermore, leaders who prioritize ethical decision-making and integrity inspire their teams to uphold those same values. This creates a culture of trust and respect, where unethical behaviors that can lead to stress and discord are less likely to flourish.

Empathy is yet another critical aspect of leading by example. Leaders who strive to understand the personal and professional challenges their team members face, and who offer support and flexibility when needed, cultivate a compassionate workplace. This approach not only decreases stress but also fosters strong, supportive relationships among team members.

Leading by example also means being proactive about your own and your team's mental health. Leaders who encourage open discussions about stress, mental health, and work-life balance, and who provide resources and support for these issues, demonstrate that it's not just work performance that matters – the well-being of the team is equally important.

Leading by example is not merely a leadership style; it's a philosophy that, when embraced, can transform an organization. It's about walking the talk, in every sense, and setting a tone that promotes a healthy, positive, and productive work environment. This isn't achieved overnight, but through consistent, genuine efforts to embody the qualities you wish to see in your team. In doing so, leaders can significantly reduce work-related stress and pave the way for a more balanced, motivated, and happy workforce.

Remember, the impact of leading by example extends far beyond the immediate team; it influences the entire organization, shaping its culture, values, and success. It's a powerful tool for creating an environment where everyone feels empowered, valued, and part of something meaningful. This, in turn, fosters happiness, productivity, and a strong sense of belonging, contributing to not just a successful organization, but a thriving one.

Encouraging Team Wellness Within the bustling life of modern work environments, the wellness of a team doesn't merely rest on the shoulders of individual members but is a collective ambition that requires nurturing and active engagement from everyone. Team wellness is akin to a garden; it thrives on consistent care, the right environment, and a communal spirit where each member contributes to the growth and well-being of others. Let's explore how to foster this nurturing environment that encourages not just individual wellness but a healthy, vibrant team spirit.

Understanding the relationship between individual wellness and team dynamics is crucial. When a team member flourishes, their enthusiasm, productivity, and positivity can be contagious, contributing to a more dynamic and vibrant team environment. Conversely, when a team leans into the culture of supporting each other, it provides a safety net for individuals going through tough times, ensuring no one is left to fend for themselves during challenging periods.

Creating a culture of open communication is the bedrock on which team wellness is built. Encouraging team members to openly discuss their stresses, challenges, and feelings without fear of judgment or retribution fosters a sense of belonging and support. It is crucial for leaders to lead by example in this realm, sharing their own experiences and vulnerabilities to normalize these conversations.

Introducing wellness activities can be a game-changer for team dynamics. These could range from group meditation sessions, yoga classes, team sports days, or wellness workshops focusing on stress management and mindfulness. The key is to find activities that resonate with team members and encourage participation without making it feel like another work obligation.

Flexibility in work arrangements can significantly impact team wellness. Allowing team members to have a say in their work schedules, offering remote work options, or considering four-day work weeks can contribute to a significant reduction in stress levels, leading to happier and more productive teams.

Recognition and appreciation play a crucial role in enhancing team wellness. Regularly acknowledging the efforts and achievements of team members, both publicly and privately, can boost morale and motivation. This doesn't always have to be grand gestures; even small tokens of appreciation can make a big difference in how valued team members feel.

Encouraging continuous personal and professional development is another key pillar. When individuals feel they are growing and learning, they are more engaged and satisfied with their work. Team development days, learning resources allowances, or encouraging attendance at conferences can all contribute to this aspect of team wellness.

Conflict resolution practices are essential in maintaining team harmony and wellness. Implementing strategies and training on conflict resolution helps ensure disputes are resolved constructively, preventing stress and negativity from permeating the team atmosphere.

Investing in the physical environment where your team works can also significantly impact wellness. Ensuring the workplace is comfortable, safe, and reflective of the team's culture can enhance the overall team spirit. Simple changes like improved lighting, comfortable seating, or the introduction of plants can make a significant difference.

Creating team traditions or rituals can foster a strong sense of community and belonging, which is vital for team wellness. Monthly team lunches, celebrating team achievements, or annual team-building retreats are just a few examples of how teams can create shared experiences that enhance their bond.

Providing a platform for health and wellness resources, such as access to counseling services, wellness apps, or subscriptions to fitness centers, shows the team that their well-being is a priority. Making these resources readily available can empower team members to take proactive steps towards their own wellness.

Encouraging regular breaks and vacations is necessary for preventing burnout and maintaining productivity. Teams should cultivate an environment where taking time off is not only accepted but encouraged, reinforcing the importance of rest and recuperation.

Developing a wellness committee within the team can provide a structured way to organize, advocate, and monitor wellness initiatives. This committee can serve as a bridge between the team and management, ensuring wellness remains a priority in decision-making processes.

Continual assessment and adaptation of wellness strategies are vital. Gathering regular feedback from team members on wellness initiatives, and being open to making changes based on this feedback, ensures that efforts remain relevant and effective. This iterative process underscores a commitment to evolving and improving team wellness continually.

Encouraging team wellness is an ongoing journey, not a destination. It requires commitment, creativity, and collaboration from all team members. By investing in a culture that places wellness at its core, teams can not only enhance their productivity and satisfaction but also enrich their professional and personal lives, creating a more harmonious, resilient, and vibrant workplace.

Building a Supportive Community Within the ecosystem of a positive workplace culture, the creation of a supportive community stands paramount. It's not merely about rallying the troops when the going gets tough; it's intricately weaving a safety net of understanding, respect, and encouragement, ensuring that no one feels they are walking their work journey alone.

The cornerstone of building such a community is open and transparent communication. It's essential to foster an environment where individuals feel confident and safe to express their thoughts, ideas, and concerns without fear of judgment or retribution. This openness can be cultivated through regular, informal team meetings, suggestion boxes, and one-on-one check-ins, ensuring that every member of the team has a voice and feels heard.

Recognition plays a vital role in nurturing a supportive atmosphere. Celebrating both the big wins and the small victories sends a powerful message of appreciation, helping to boost morale and motivation. A simple gesture, like a personalized thank you note for a job well done, can significantly impact someone's sense of belonging and value within the team.

Another fundamental aspect is the cultivation of mutual respect among coworkers. This involves providing opportunities for team members to learn about each other's roles, challenges, and contributions to the team's success. Understanding each other's workloads and pressures helps in fostering patience and empathy, thereby strengthening the bonds within the community.

Empathy and kindness should not just be buzzwords but core components of the company culture. This could mean implementing policies that support work-life balance, such as flexible work hours or remote working options. It could also manifest through mental health days or providing access to wellness resources, highlighting the organization's commitment to its members' well-being.

Mentorship programs can greatly augment the sense of support within a workplace. Pairing less experienced employees with seasoned professionals can facilitate skill development and career growth, while also strengthening inter-personal relationships. Such programs signal an investment in employees' professional development, reinforcing their value to the organization.

Creating a sense of community also involves inclusive decision-making. This means involving team members in brainstorming sessions, solution finding, and strategic planning. It validates their contributions and showcases trust in their judgment and abilities, fostering a sense of ownership and accountability.

At the same time, providing constructive feedback is crucial. It should be aimed at promoting growth and learning rather than casting blame. Equipping leaders and managers with the right tools and training to give effective feedback can make all the difference in maintaining a positive and supportive workplace.

Encouraging social interactions outside the official work setting can also fortify relationships within the team. Organizing team-building activities, volunteer opportunities, or simple social gatherings allows individuals to connect on a more personal level, developing friendships that strengthen the support system at work.

Handling conflicts with sensitivity and neutrality is another critical component. Conflicts, when managed poorly, can disrupt the community's fabric, but when addressed promptly and fairly, can lead to improved understanding and teamwork. Offering training in conflict resolution or having a clear, transparent process in place for handling disputes can help maintain harmony.

Moreover, soliciting and acting upon feedback from team members shows that their opinions are valued and considered in decision-making. This doesn't only pertain to work-related matters but extends to the community aspects, such as the effectiveness of support systems and inclusivity efforts. An environment that adapts based on feedback is one that grows stronger and more cohesive over time.

On a larger scale, organizations should strive to create partnerships with other companies, non-profits, and community organizations. These relationships can provide employees with additional support resources, learning opportunities, and avenues for community service, further enriching the sense of purpose and connection within the workplace.

Finally, leadership must embody the values they wish to see in their team. Leaders who demonstrate empathy, inclusiveness, and a genuine concern for their team's well-being set the tone for the entire organization. Their actions and attitudes are powerful motivators for others to do the same, creating a ripple effect of support and positivity throughout the workplace.

Building a supportive community within the workplace is not a one-time effort but a continuous process of nurturing the emotional and professional well-being of every individual. It's about creating a space where everyone feels valued, respected, and an integral part of the team. When people come together in such an environment, not only do they thrive individually, but they propel the organization to new heights of success and fulfillment.

The journey towards cultivating this kind of community might be fraught with challenges, but the rewards—in terms of increased productivity, job satisfaction, and overall happiness—are immeasurable. By aiming for a supportive workplace community, organizations can unlock the full potential of their teams and foster an environment where everyone looks forward to coming to work each day.

Conclusion

As we conclude this journey together, it's important to reflect on the transformation that has unfolded across these pages. We've traversed the complex terrain of work stress, discovering its anatomy and identifying personal triggers. We've equipped ourselves with a multitude of strategies, from managing overwhelming feelings to achieving a gracious balance between work and life. Now, at the culmination of this guide, it's essential to look ahead, understanding that the path to well-being is both continuous and evolving.

Tackling work stress and fostering happiness in our professional lives is an ongoing process, not a destination. It requires patience, commitment, and a gentle acknowledgment of our progress and setbacks. Every technique and approach we've explored opens the door to a more balanced, productive, and fulfilling work experience. However, the real magic happens when these strategies become part of your daily routine, seamlessly integrating into your life as habits that support your well-being.

Remember, the concept of balance shifts with the sands of time and the changing tides of our lives. What constitutes balance today may need adjustment tomorrow. Thus, flexibility and self-compassion become our greatest allies. As we embrace the ever-changing nature of work environments, learning new skills, and adapting to change positively becomes imperative for maintaining resilience and a future-focused mindset.

In cultivating a positive workplace culture, remember that the influence begins with you. Leading by example and encouraging team wellness can spark a transformation that contributes to a supportive community. This not only enhances your happiness at work but also radiates to those around you, creating ripples of positive change in the broader workplace environment.

It's also crucial to continuously seek alignment with your personal and professional values, connecting your work to your fundamental 'why.' This alignment acts as a compass, guiding your decisions, motivating your efforts, and providing a sense of fulfillment that transcends the ordinary metrics of success.

As you move forward, your personal stress-management plan will be your roadmap, yet it's vital to remain open to adjusting its course. Regular self-assessment allows you to tweak your strategies, ensuring they continue to serve your evolving needs. Life throws curveballs, and what worked yesterday may not be as effective today. Agility in your approach to well-being is your key to staying balanced through life's fluctuations.

One of the most powerful takeaways is the importance of cultivating connections—whether it's seeking support from peers and mentors, navigating interpersonal challenges, or advocating for yourself and your ideas. Relationships can be both a source of stress and a powerful conduit for stress relief. It's the quality of these connections that often defines our work experience.

Always remember, stress is not inherently negative. It's our response to stress that can lead to growth or discomfort. Viewing challenges as opportunities for growth fosters a resilience that not only aids in stress management but also in personal and professional development.

The journey to happiness at work is inherently personal. No single strategy fits all, and the beauty of this journey lies in discovering what uniquely works for you. This book has armed you with a plethora of tools and insights, but the real work begins with application and experimentation in your own life.

Finally, take a moment to acknowledge your commitment to seeking happiness and balance in your professional life. This commitment itself is a major step toward achieving the well-being you deserve. Happiness at work is not just about reducing stress; it's about creating an environment where you can thrive, feel valued, and contribute your best.

May this book serve as a beacon on your path, illuminating the way forward as you navigate the complexities of the working world with grace, resilience, and an unwavering commitment to your well-being.

As we part ways, I encourage you to keep exploring, learning, and growing. The pursuit of happiness at work is a journey that continues well beyond the pages of this book. Let your curiosity and desire for well-being be the guiding lights as you forge your path to a fulfilling and balanced professional life.

In closing, we return to where we began, with an understanding that the key to happiness at work lies within our power to shape our perceptions, responses, and the environment we cultivate. Armed with the knowledge and strategies from this guide, you are now better equipped to navigate the challenges and opportunities that come your way, creating a work-life that not only sustains you but allows you to flourish.

Here's to your journey toward happiness at work—may it be revealing, rewarding, and rich with growth. Thank you for allowing me to be a part of this significant chapter in your professional life.

Appendix A: Additional Resources for Managing Work Stress

As we've journeyed together through the insights and strategies to aid you in managing work stress, it's essential to arm you with a toolkit that extends beyond the covers of this book. Exploring additional resources can provide you with a broader perspective and deeper understanding, empowering you to tailor your stress-management approach to fit your unique needs. In this appendix, we'll introduce you to a variety of resources, including recommended reading, cutting-edge stress-management apps and tools, and professional organizations dedicated to stress and well-being.

A.1: Recommended Reading

Immersing yourselves in enlightening literature can transform the way you perceive and handle work stress. Here's a list of books that delve into various aspects of stress management, resilience building, and finding joy in your daily work:

- **Redefining Mondays: Pathways to Work-Life Harmony by Leah DeMarest-** guides you through understanding the root causes of your Monday disheartenment and provides you with actionable solutions to foster an enduring sense of fulfillment and happiness in your professional and personal life.

- **Resilience: Hard-Won Wisdom for Living a Better Life by Eric Greitens** - Explores the concept of resilience and how it can be cultivated to face life's challenges with strength and grace.

- **The Upside of Stress: Why Stress Is Good for You, and How to Get Good at It by Kelly McGonigal** - Offers a refreshing perspective on stress, suggesting that embracing stress can lead to personal growth and happiness.

- **Mindfulness for Beginners: Reclaiming the Present Moment—and Your Life by Jon Kabat-Zinn-** A practical guide for integrating mindfulness into your daily life to enhance presence and reduce stress.

A.1: Recommended Reading (continued)

In the journey toward mastering your work stress, broadening your perspective can make all the difference. The right book doesn't just impart knowledge; it can resonate with your soul, nudge you towards introspection, and equip you with the tools to face your challenges head-on. That's why we've carefully curated a reading list that promises to enlighten, inspire, and transform your approach to work, stress, and the elusive balance we all seek between the two.

First on our list is a book that I authored that will give you a blueprint for not just combating the Monday Blues but also for enhancing your motivation, focus, and job satisfaction throughout the week. Through practical strategies you will learn how to kickstart your week with positivity, obtain adequate sleep, a nourishing diet, and exercises that boost mood and energy. *Redefining Mondays* offers a comprehensive approach to reimagining the very essence of work and its place in a balanced, joyful life.

Next on the list is a book that peels back the layers of work-induced stress, offering not just insights but also actionable techniques to manage and mitigate these feelings. It delves into the art of mindful living, suggesting that the key to stress resolution lies in the moment-to-moment awareness of our thoughts, actions, and reactions. Through a combination of empirical evidence and relatable anecdotes, this read promises to be both educational and engaging.

The next recommendation explores the concept of resilience in the workplace. It's a compelling narrative that intertwines the latest research with powerful stories from professionals who've thrived against all odds. This book doesn't just tell you to 'be resilient'—it shows you how. It breaks down resilience into a series of traits and habits that can be cultivated over time, offering a roadmap to not just bounce back from setbacks but to leap forward.

Emotional intelligence at work is another cornerstone of managing work stress effectively, and so, our list includes a groundbreaking book on this very topic. It argues that emotional intelligence is the linchpin of professional success and personal well-being, providing a new paradigm through which to view and interact with others in the workplace. The book is replete with strategies to enhance your emotional intelligence, thereby transforming your work relationships and environment.

Nurturing a positive work-life balance is crucial, and so we recommend a book that tackles this challenge directly. It's a refreshing take on how to delineate and prioritize the competing interests of your personal and professional life. With practical exercises and real-life examples, it guides you through setting boundaries and creating a life that's fulfilling both in and out of the office.

In the realm of productivity, we have selected a book that challenges the status quo of 'busyness'. It's a deep dive into the cult of productivity, questioning the relentless pursuit of more. Instead, it offers an alternative philosophy centered on doing less, but better. This book is an essential read for anyone looking to reclaim their time, focus, and joy in their work.

To complement the practical aspects of stress management, our list wouldn't be complete without a book on the science of happiness at work. Mixing robust scientific research with accessible writing, it explores how our brains work best and how we can leverage this understanding to create more joy in our work. It's a testament to the fact that happiness and productivity are not mutually exclusive but rather go hand in hand.

For those seeking to master the digital tools that can streamline work and reduce stress, we recommend a book on the smart use of technology in the workplace. It covers everything from managing your inbox to leveraging project management apps to free up mental space and energy for the work that truly matters.

Navigating the complexities of interpersonal relationships at work can be a significant source of stress. That's why our list includes a guide on managing difficult conversations. It's packed with strategies for engaging in dialogue that's both productive and respectful, transforming potential conflicts into opportunities for growth.

Leadership, too, has a pivotal role in shaping workplace culture and stress levels. Thus, a book on compassionate leadership is on our list, offering insights into fostering a work environment that values wellness and empathy as much as it does productivity.

Finally, understanding the physiological impact of stress is crucial for managing it effectively. We recommend a book that bridges the gap between mind and body, detailing how stress affects our physical health and what we can do to mitigate these effects. This book combines cutting-edge research with practical advice, making it an invaluable resource for anyone looking to live a healthier, more balanced life.

Including these titles in your personal library will not only enhance your understanding of work stress and its many facets but also empower you with the knowledge and skills to tackle it head-on. Reading is a form of self-care, a way to momentarily step away from the hustle and recharge, armed with new insights and perspectives. So, we encourage you to dive into these recommended reads, and let them guide you towards a more balanced, joyful, and productive life.

Remember, the journey to managing work stress is ongoing, and there's always more to learn and explore. These books are your companions on this journey, shedding light on paths you might not have considered and equipping you with the tools to navigate your work life with grace and resilience. Happy reading!

A.2: Stress-Management Apps and Tools

In today's digital age, technology offers innovative solutions to manage stress efficiently. Here are some apps and tools designed to provide stress relief, improve mental health, and boost productivity:

- **Headspace** - Offers guided meditations, sleep sounds, and mindfulness exercises to reduce stress and improve overall well-being.
- **Calm** - Features a wide array of mindfulness exercises, including guided meditations, breathing techniques, and sleep stories.
- **Forest** - Encourages focused work sessions and reduces phone usage by letting you grow virtual trees every time you stay away from your smartphone.

A.2: Stress-Management Apps and Tools (continued) In today's fast-paced work environment, stress is as inevitable as the next email notification. While we've explored many hands-on techniques to tame the turbulence of workplace pressures, technology can be a formidable ally in this crusade. The magic of stress-management apps and tools unfolds through their ability to personalize, track, and engage users in practices proven to down-regulate stress responses and foster well-being. Let's navigate this digital landscape together, pinpointing the applications that can be your pocket-sized peacekeepers.

The tranquility of a mindfulness session or the vigor of a quick workout is no further than a tap away with today's technology. Stress-management apps leverage the principles of psychology and neurology, making therapeutic techniques accessible anytime, anywhere. Whether it's through guided meditation, breathing exercises, or habit-tracking, these apps can be a seamless part of your daily routine, offering a refuge from the workday whirlwind.

Consider meditation apps, for instance. They are not just about closing your eyes and floating away into oblivion. These digital guides can introduce you to mindfulness practices in bite-sized sessions, perfect for a lunch break or a quick pause between meetings. From increasing focus to enhancing emotional resilience, the multifaceted benefits of meditation have been praised far and wide. With customizable sessions based on your current stress levels and goals, these apps can be your personal meditation coach.

Breathing exercises are another cornerstone of stress management, and thankfully, there's an app for that too. These tools teach and remind you to engage in deep, diaphragmatic breathing, a practice that can quickly shift your body from a stress-induced fight-or-flight mode to a more relaxed state. By incorporating regular breathing exercises into your day, preferably with the guidance and structure provided by an app, you can develop a powerful antidote to workplace stress.

Exercise apps also make the cut when we talk about beating stress. Physical activity is a scientifically proven stress-buster, and with apps offering everything from high-intensity interval training (HIIT) sessions to yoga flows, getting your daily dose of endorphins has never been easier. Tailored to fit into busy schedules, these apps can remind you to stay active, track your progress, and even provide virtual communities for a dose of social support.

Journaling apps deserve a mention too. Reflecting on your day, penning down worries, and journaling about gratitude can be profoundly therapeutic. Digital journaling apps offer the added benefits of privacy, convenience, and even mood tracking. Over time, you can observe patterns in your stress triggers and responses, gaining insights that are instrumental in managing stress more effectively.

Then there's the realm of habit-tracking apps, which can play a pivotal role in your stress-management toolkit. Whether it's committing to daily meditation, regular exercise, or setting aside time for hobbies, tracking your habits can boost accountability and provide clear insights into your progress. These apps often gamify the experience, making the journey towards a less stressed life not just rewarding but fun.

It's crucial, however, to approach these digital tools with a strategic mindset. Not all apps are created equal, and what works for one person may not work for another. Begin by identifying your primary stressors and objectives. Are you looking to improve sleep, enhance focus, or manage anxiety? From there, explore apps that cater to these specific needs, paying close attention to user reviews and evidence-based practices behind them.

Integration into your daily routine is the key to the success of any stress-management app. Start small, maybe with a five-minute meditation or a quick journaling session in the morning. As you grow more comfortable, you can expand your digital wellness practices. Remember, consistency is more impactful than intensity when it comes to building stress resilience.

Privacy and data security should also be on your radar. As we entrust these apps with sensitive information about our health and habits, ensuring they adhere to strict data protection standards is essential. Look for transparency in how they collect, use, and protect your data before you commit to using an app.

Despite the abundance of digital tools at our disposal, technology should not be seen as a panacea for workplace stress. It's one piece of the puzzle, complemented by traditional stress-management techniques, professional support, and organizational changes aimed at reducing stressors. The goal is to create a holistic strategy that leverages the best of both worlds.

Don't overlook the potential for technological overload either. In a world where our screens often contribute to our stress, balancing digital and non-digital stress management practices is crucial. Use technology mindfully, setting boundaries to ensure your digital wellness tools are serving you, not overwhelming you.

The exploration of stress-management apps and tools is a journey of self-discovery and personalization. What resonates with one individual may not with another, and that's perfectly okay. The aim is to curate a suite of digital aids that align with your lifestyle, preferences, and stress-management needs. This process of trial and adaptation is itself an exercise in mindfulness and self-care.

Finally, remember that these tools are not just for moments of acute stress. Incorporating them into your daily routine can strengthen your resilience, making you better equipped to handle stressors when they arise. Like any skill, stress management improves with practice, and these apps can be your constant companions, coaching and cheering you on as you navigate the complexities of workplace well-being.

The landscape of stress-management apps and tools is rich and varied, offering something for everyone. From meditation to exercise, journaling to habit tracking, these digital resources can complement traditional strategies, helping you cultivate a more balanced, fulfilled work life. Embrace the journey, experiment with what works for you, and remember, in the quest for workplace happiness, you're not alone. Technology, with its vast and ever-evolving toolkit, is right there with you, ready to support your path to well-being.

A.3: Professional Organizations for Stress and Well-Being

Connecting with professionals dedicated to stress management and employee well-being can provide valuable support and resources. Here are a few organizations offering workshops, seminars, and networking opportunities:

- **American Institute of Stress (AIS)** - Dedicated to understanding and combating stress through comprehensive research and education.

- **International Stress Management Association (ISMA)** - Offers a platform for professionals to share knowledge on stress management, with chapters in various countries.

- **National Wellness Institute (NWI)** - Promotes wellness and well-being in individuals and organizations through certifications, resources, and professional development.

Empowering yourself with knowledge and tools from a variety of sources can significantly enhance your ability to manage work stress. Whether it's through diving into a compelling book, utilizing an app daily, or connecting with like-minded professionals, each step you take enriches your journey towards a balanced, fulfilling work life.

A.3: Professional Organizations for Stress and Well-Being (continued) In our journey toward mastering stress at work and achieving an admirable balance between our personal and professional lives, it's paramount to tap into the resources and support systems available to us. Professional organizations dedicated to stress management and well-being play a crucial role in providing insights, techniques, and a sense of community for those seeking to enhance their quality of life in and out of the workplace.

In the vast landscape of professional life, the stressors we encounter can often seem insurmountable. Yet, it's these very challenges that compel us to seek out camaraderie and expertise from those who've dedicated their careers to understanding and combating stress. Among the multitude of resources available, professional organizations offer a unique blend of research-based knowledge and practical strategies designed to foster well-being.

One notable example of such an entity is the American Institute of Stress (AIS). Founded with the goal of understanding and managing stress in holistic and innovative ways, AIS provides a treasure trove of information on stress reduction practices. Their resources, which range from scientific articles to stress management tools, serve to enlighten individuals on how stress affects our lives and how we can navigate these turbulent waters with greater poise and efficacy.

Similarly, the International Stress Management Association (ISMA) stands as a beacon for professionals seeking strategies to manage stress. Offering workshops, certification programs, and access to a community of experts, ISMA focuses on promoting sound stress management practices in both personal and professional spheres.

The Mindfulness Association is another key player in the realm of stress management and well-being. With its roots deeply entrenched in the practice of mindfulness, this organization offers courses, research, and events aimed at cultivating mindfulness as a foundational skill for managing stress and enhancing overall quality of life.

The incorporation of meditation and mindfulness practices into our daily routines is not merely a trend but a testament to their efficacy in managing stress. Organizations like The Center for Contemplative Mind in Society have taken this mantra to heart, focusing their efforts on integrating contemplative practices into various sectors including education, law, business, and healthcare. This approach not only assists in stress reduction but also fosters a deeper sense of connectivity and fulfillment in one's professional life.

On a somewhat different yet equally important note, the importance of physical wellness cannot be understated when talking about stress and well-being. The National Wellness Institute (NWI) champions this cause by offering resources and certification programs that emphasize the role of physical health in maintaining mental and emotional equilibrium.

For those navigating the treacherous waters of workplace well-being, the Wellness Council of America (WELCOA) provides a lighthouse in the form of best practices, research, and case studies related to workplace wellness. Their dedication to creating healthier work environments is a pivotal aspect of stress management, recognizing that organizational culture plays an instrumental role in individual stress levels.

Furthermore, the role of occupational health psychology in understanding and mitigating work-related stress has given rise to organizations like the Society for Occupational Health Psychology (SOHP). This organization delves into the science behind work stress and its solutions, offering conferences, journals, and community forums for professionals in the field.

Another vital resource is the Anxiety and Depression Association of America (ADAA), which, while not exclusively focused on work-related stress, provides extensive information and support for individuals dealing with anxiety and depression, conditions often exacerbated by or manifesting as a result of workplace stress.

The Work Stress and Health Conference, co-sponsored by the American Psychological Association (APA), the National Institute for Occupational Safety and Health (NIOSH), and the Society for Occupational Health Psychology (SOHP), stands as a testament to the collective effort aimed at understanding and combatting work-related stress. By congregating experts and practitioners from various fields, the conference fosters an environment of learning and exchange aimed at innovative solutions for work stress management.

Engagement with such organizations not only enriches our understanding and toolkit for managing stress but also instills a sense of belonging to a broader community that shares our challenges and aspirations. The value of these professional organizations extends beyond their archives of knowledge, embodying a collective endeavor to enhance well-being in the professional realm.

Despite the wealth of resources these organizations offer, it's crucial for individuals to proactively seek out and engage with the knowledge and communities they provide. By doing so, we empower ourselves to navigate stress with resilience, turning what once may have seemed like insurmountable obstacles into manageable hurdles.

In essence, the journey toward optimal well-being and stress management in our professional lives is one that we don't have to undertake alone. Professional organizations dedicated to stress and well-being serve as allies in this endeavor, offering guidance, support, and a sense of community to those seeking to thrive in the face of work-related challenges. As we move forward in our careers, let us lean on the wisdom and resources these organizations offer, cultivating a healthier, more balanced approach to work and life.

Ultimately, embracing the support and expertise of these professional organizations can significantly contribute to our journey towards a happier, more balanced work life. By integrating their insights and practices into our daily routines, we have the opportunity to transform our professional environments into spaces of growth, balance, and well-being.

Milton Keynes UK
Ingram Content Group UK Ltd.
UKHW020405021124
450424UK00014B/1442